MELISSA MALIKOWSKI

HOPE
is a
FOUR-LETTER
WORD

Twenty
Literary Group

Hope is a Four-Letter Word
Copyright © 2025 by Melissa Malikowski

Library of Congress Control Number: 2025900930

ISBN
978-1-964488-50-9 (Paperback)
978-1-964488-51-6 (eBook)
978-1-964488-49-3 (Hardcover)

Dedication

J. Know that you are EPIC. Know who/what is a blessing in your life and know who/what is a lesson. Know what's worth going for in life and what's worth letting go. That is the key to life. You are worth SO MUCH more than what she could EVER offer you. Know that I GOT YOU!

I care about you so much and I meant every written word. I can guarantee you I can back up what I wrote 150 billion times the national debt which just keeps growing.

Simply, no one compares to you. Some people/things are worth waiting for. I'm waiting for you and I'd wait an eternity, if needed. You are totally worth the wait. There simply isn't anyone else on this earth that compares to you.

Laila: My sister on so many levels. You are such a blessing. I'm so happy for you. You so deserve this. I will be at your event with BELLS on. I love you, my sister.

To my team: AA, DF, TK, DK, TL, LM, YM, MN. You are ALL so EPIC. I love you, my team. Thank you for your support when horrible things happened. I'm so grateful to all of you for your love and support.

The 3 David's in my life: I'm so GRATEFUL for all of you. Know that you have changed my life for the better. Thank you all. All of you mean the WORLD to me.

To My Boys (My nephews): You both have turned into fine young men. Your mother decided not to pass on the trauma we endured. She decided she could do better. She did along with your father. Way to go gentlemen! You've made me so proud of you. I love you both so much.

To SURVIVORS of narcissistic abuse: Know you are not alone. You are worth fighting for. Do NOT let the ASS destroy you. They TOTALLY will. Know when to walk. Draw a line. If the ass goes one centimeter over it. WALK. Grab what's yours and don't let the door hit you on the ass on the way out. I BELEVE IN YOU! You're worth SO much more. YOU GOT THIS!

Table of Contents

Life wasn't ever roses for me, but when is it ever? For 32 years, I was an emotional, physical and mental wreck. I really was a terrible person. I backstabbed, I gossiped, I was a bully, I thought I was the shit when in reality I was a coward. I thought I knew everything. Really, I knew shit. I still do.

Whatever you may want to call me, please do not call me a victim. I'm a survivor. I have choices and power over my behavior. I take responsibility for my actions in life. Have I messed up and made some really, really bad choices: yes. I take full, personal responsibility for those I've caused any pain, suffering or embarrassment.

As I get older, I realize I know less and less about the world and my place in it. I was so certain about everything when I was young. Now, I know nothing in life is for certain. I could get hit by a Mack truck tomorrow and never finish this book. Unlikely, but it still could happen. Do I fear going out of the house because of it? No! My aim is to live life to the best of my ability. I lost 32 years of my life to mental illness and a binge eating disorder. I do not want to waste a second of what I have left.

I got really, really angry on New Year's Eve 2019. I was sitting in my La-Z-Boy chair hating my life. Not just hating it, but taking a really good look at myself and seeing that I really didn't like what I saw. I saw an obese, lazy, pre-diabetic, boke person who was really unhappy. I liked the idea of a pill fixing everything until I didn't. I wanted to do something about it.

So, I made a few decisions: to get my finances in order, to get to a gym, to start caring about my health, what I ate and to stop being a horrible person. This was before COVID hit. I made it to the gym 10 times that January. Enough to get most of my membership paid by my health plan. I also lost 5 pounds. At the time, I was 240 pounds. I was starting slow to say the least, but at least I was starting. That is more than some people.

This was the beginning of truly facing my past, my trauma, taking a good look in the mirror and saying that I wanted to be a better version of myself. Version 1.0 had too many issues, sucked, was severely broken and was a total fake.

I had to build version 2.0. This would take a metamorphosis of extreme proportions. The road actually started in 2006 but had been stalled for quite awhile. I wanted to be different. I wanted to be the person I was meant to be on this earth-an honestly, good human being.

I'm not saying I was going to walk on water. No one is perfect. I just wanted to heal, essentially, and be the person God, the Universe or whoever intended me to be. I no longer wanted to be this fake, unhappy, unhealthy person I was.

I wanted to be beautiful inside and out, a woman who lit up a room when she entered it, whose smile radiated and who emitted positive energy that lifts people up wherever she went. She would come, but later in life.

You can't see where I'm going or how I continue to improve until you've seen all the trauma I've made it through that molded me into the strong, confident, loving person I am today.

My story starts or my previous life ended in an emergency room in 2006 where most of the "old me" died. I had a job I absolutely hated. My boss was an abusive person. I was an emotional and mental wreck. His abuse made things a million times worse.

I hated Mondays and lived for Fridays. I was trying to find a new position within the university but no one wants to hire a desperate, needy person. I missed so much work because I simply couldn't make it out of bed as I was so depressed. Medications did nothing as I was so low at the time.

I hated myself and my life so much. I lived by myself and I was calling my therapist every day. I needed him to help me cope with a life I hated, a job I hated and to save me from a person I hated…me. My doctor is a saint and I owe him much more than I could ever earn in 10 lifetimes, even if I were a billionaire.

One day in September, I called and I talked to his nurse. She asked me one question: "Are you going to hurt yourself?" At that moment, I honestly didn't know. I didn't know what I was capable of, and I knew I was scared to death of dying in the apartment alone with no one there to save me should something happen.

The thoughts of death were becoming a welcome solution to my never-ending pain. Needless to say, she asked if I had anyone that could bring me to the hospital. I called my mom to see if she could take me. She told me she didn't know the way to my apartment as if Mapquest didn't exist.

I guess if that were me, and my child were suicidal, I'd fight fire, climb mountains and swim the seven seas to get to them. However, we're talking about my mother here. She is more into what makes her comfortable and happy.

Anyone else simply doesn't matter. This has been a scene that has played out my entire life. I, again, was on my own. My dad didn't even come home from work early that day.

She told me to call the ambulance which I did and that she and my dad would come during visiting hours. Somehow, that didn't make me feel any better or supported. I felt more alone than ever. Yet again, I was left to hang and I was scared.

I packed my suitcase and waited for the ambulance to arrive. I was so ashamed of myself. My life was over. The only thought I had was "My God! I've hit rock bottom." There's nowhere else to go from here. I would either go up, or die. I knew I just couldn't live this way anymore.

The ambulance ride was the loneliest ride with the paramedics asking me questions like what brings you in today and what are your symptoms? Are you taking your meds? What meds are you taking?

The 8 hours in the ER were the worst 8 hours of my life. I was totally and completely alone. I spent it curled in a ball, crying and begging God to save me. I made a deal; I would live a better life, get my depression and borderline personality disorder under control if God would help me be the person I was meant to be. It would only take 18 years. It was a very slow process. I was 28 when I went into the hospital. I guess it's better late than never.

I wanted to live differently, and have a life worth living. I wanted to know what happiness and actual love were and felt like. The experience and the path would be filled with anger, resentment, extreme mental anguish and trauma. I would face some of the most painful, agonizing and rewarding moments in my journey back to mental wellness.

I had to look in the mirror and see and face things I'd done and the painful things that happened to me. It was so painful and freeing all at the same time.

However, with the pain came peace, letting go of the trauma and understanding that life isn't like a movie. My life certainly wasn't. If it was, mine was a terrible crap drama that was never-ending like movies on the Lifetime Movie Network.

At times life was like having your heart ripped out of your chest, put on a stake, arrows piercing through it, having it burned and the ashes stomped on and thrown in the back of a garbage truck. I felt so worthless and that life had somehow left me behind.

I've made mistakes, messed up and fell off the wagon to betterment several times, but I always made the choice, no matter how difficult it was, to get back on. I've picked myself off the shit stained, smelly floor so many times the smell and the stains don't bother me anymore.

I rise. I've learned to bear my crosses and carry them up mountains. Maybe, even Everest. I've borne crosses that weren't mine to bear but I still carried them...until I threw them off and gave the burden or responsibility to the true owners. The shame wasn't mine. It never was.

I've been cheated on, lied to, used, taken for granted, scapegoated, taught to be pleasing and forced to be a parent to my parents. I also raised my mother while raising myself. Oh, and my ex-husband impregnated another woman while we were married. He also claimed it was my fault. This shit was toxic and I had a LOT of work to do, personally.

However, I made it and I am honestly completely amazed and proud of the person I have become. The road wasn't easy but it proves that horrible past and present circumstances do not predict a bad future. This is my story of survival and rebirth.

THE EARLY YEARS

I grew up in a working class family in Minneapolis, Minnesota. My mom was a nurse and worked for a hospital and my dad was an electrician for the railroad.

The memories I have of early childhood were somewhat happy. We were like the perfect family…until we weren't.

In the early 80's, my mother injured her back at the hospital lifting a patient and couldn't work on the floor she was on anymore. She had requested to go to a lighter lifting floor. Because her employer was so great, they laid her off or terminated her.

I honestly don't remember most of the details, but I do know she had to get a lawyer. They eventually put her on the OB floor. Things went downhill from there. My parents argued constantly about money. Being the little 6 year old that I was, I would become so scared when they would fight.

One day I asked my dad if we were going to have to leave and be homeless. Being the sensitive father he was, he told me that I should get a job. He was kidding, but it really wasn't funny to me. I had heard several nasty fights between the two of them.

My mother liked to spend freely and unwisely buying whatever her heart desired. My dad hated spending money-especially on my sister and I. Each argument put me on edge as a child and I took it upon myself to try to make it better. There would be several such incidents in the years to come.

I worried about many things as a 6-year-old. Really, these were not things a child should be worried about at that age. I would go through my childhood and teenage years acting older than my years with responsibilities of an adult at a very young age. I grew up before my time. My childhood ended at age six.

On the night before my first day of kindergarten, I remember asking my dad how to make friends. He told me that if I was a good girl and I smiled, people would be nice to me. Do. Not. Ever give a child that advice! It's terrible advice.

He also taught me that if someone is nice to you, they like you and they must be a good person? Again, don't tell your child that, either. Serial killers, child abusers, psychopaths and narcissists are "really nice" too.

It's just they will either kill you so they are the last "friend" you ever have or they will abuse you, gaslight you, suck your well dry and blame you for being traumatized because of it. Cause' nothing is their fault.

Got me one of those types later in life. Needless to say, I don't follow that advice and it took me years to figure out that just because someone was nice to me, it doesn't mean they are a good person. It was a very hard lesson to learn.

So I went to Kindergarten, smiled and was a good girl. It got me a bully who liked to make me cry. He did that a lot. I would have a lot of bully's growing up. Unfortunately, I would eventually turn into one myself.

I was really an emotionally sensitive child. It happens when you don't feel safe in your own environment or even secure in who you are. Things affected me more than they should have. Mom was always telling me that I was too sensitive and that I needed a thicker skin.

I was blamed for being bullied and I thought it was my fault. My own mother and the teachers I had told me the same line of bullshit like that the boys wouldn't be mean to me if I wouldn't cry. I guess it was too much of a hassle to punish or have consequences for the bullies or to stop it all together. After all, it was my fault that they were horribly mean, not theirs?

What my parents should have taught me is that I needed to stick up for myself, how not to be used and how to recognize when I was being taken advantage of. They did not teach me these things. Instead, I would lose my self-esteem and self-worth early on. I grew up feeling like I had no power and that I was ugly and worthless. Those were lessons that cost me dearly in life.

I was a good kid and I remember starting to fear things early on and having bad anxiety. I worried about everything, death, not fitting in, failing a grade (grades weren't even given at that time it was S/N), losing my friends, being homeless, where my next meal was coming from and we had food at that time.

Basically, I worried about things a child of 6 or 7 shouldn't be worried about. I would talk to my parents about it, and they would push it off as if I didn't know what I was talking about. This would be a red flag early on. They missed it.

I asked my mom one day after having a bath if I was going to Hell when I die. I was in first grade! She asked why I thought that, and I told her because I was a bad kid. For some reason this did not cause a huge red flag in her mind.

One of many red flags that she and my dad would miss while I was growing up. I thought I was a bad kid that God couldn't even love. If that doesn't flash "Danger" in some way in a parent, nothing will.

I was cute and my cousins thought I was a good child to have as the baby if we were playing house. This was until I wasn't cute anymore and my mom lost interest in taking care of my sister and I. She just stopped being a mom. I don't think I would recognize the mother of my early years if she ever came back, as she has been gone for so long.

When I was in kindergarten, my mom insisted on doing my hair and dressing me as cute as she could. I had to have ponytails. My hair was longer, very thick and was naturally curly. She would sit me on a stool while taking a fine toothed comb and ripping it down the back of my head.

She would pull my hair, I would cry and scream as it hurt….a lot. She would just get madder and pull more and harder. My sister would watch helplessly as I cried and screamed. This would go on until mom lost interest in taking care of us.

All of a sudden, in second grade, I was responsible for brushing my hair, knowing what to wear to school and knowing when to take a bath. I was too young for this and my sister didn't know how to care for me-not that I expected that of her at that time.

Luckily, dad was home usually at night to give me a bath so we didn't look neglected. However, we were neglected, ignored and I was emotionally and mentally neglected and emotionally abused. Somehow my sister wasn't as bad off as I was at the time.

My sister has always been my Dad's favorite and still is to this day. The things he let happen to me at her hands were cruel and just painful. My sister suffered too. I don't doubt that, but both my parents were and still are emotionally immature and narcissistic. I wouldn't learn this until much later in life.

I was the child that my dad wanted the least. I was two years early as they wanted my sister to be 4 when they had another baby. Well…accidents happen. I arrive two years early, unplanned.

My dad was NOT happy that I came early and was a total ass while my mom was pregnant.

When I was born, much to my mother's discontent, I preferred my dad as a baby. I would stop crying if dad held me.

Again, my sister is his favorite. He will tell me that's not true but his actions speak louder than his words.

The child my dad wanted the least, loved him the most.

We were called "Brats" threatened with having our heads banged together which happened during a car ride. We were fighting about something and my Dad reached back and slammed our heads together all while driving.

He didn't even miss a beat or almost get us into an accident. My mom, after seeing that, did tell him to never do that again. He never did, but he would slap my sister if she talked back as would my mom. I learned quickly what not to do based on what happened to my sister. I would learn how to be the "perfect" child.

Being called a "brat" was common and I was also called a "pest" whenever I wanted something. We couldn't have new toys unless it was Christmas or our birthday. Dad would get seriously pissed if mom bought toys for us outside of those two occasions.

Because of this, if mom bought something for us like a toy, we would have to "hide" it. This was considered "normal" in my world. Dad thought we were "spoiled brats." He could be such an asshole when we were really young.

Growing up I was not enrolled in sports, kids clubs or anything like that. My sister was in Brownies which I think was the group before the Girlscouts at the time. However, my mom didn't want to assist with the group.

She was more of a "I drop my kid off and leave" sort of parent. She never wanted to help with the events or involve herself with the other parents. Dad didn't want to drive my sister to the group when mom worked. Dad was into taking a nap after work and not into caring about taking his daughters to anything that would take away from his nap time. That venture ended rather quickly.

My sister was also in dance, but she hated it. In first grade, I was enrolled in Junior Chefs that lasted about 3 weeks and taught us how to use a new, fandangled thing called a microwave. And how to make such healthy meals as a hotdog in a Pillsbury croissant.

I was never enrolled in anything after that. Had I been enrolled in kids groups it probably could have helped my shyness assisted with self-esteem and self-worth. We were sent to before and after school daycare at school but that ended up being too expensive, so they had the woman who lived on the corner of our street take care of us. She watch us until my sister was old enough to look after me.

There was a babysitter on the other side of us who did take care of us up until we switched. My parents discovered that she was spanking us hard enough to leave bruises. One day my sister was playing with the playground equipment in the sitter's back yard, and fell into a puddle. The sitter thought she had wet her pants and spanked her hard enough to leave bruises.

I remember watching it even to this day. I remember what the paddle looked like and that my sister never cried. I remember the look of defiance she had on her face as she was being hit.

She would take a beating that day but she would not give the sitter the satisfaction of seeing her cry. She would have to stay in the corner also. She sat there and snapped the gum she was chewing just to annoy the sitter. She achieved her goal, but nothing further happened to her that day.

When we were set in for bath time that night, my mom saw the horrific bruises and asked my sister where they came from. My sister told her that the sitter had paddled her for falling into a puddle. To say my mom was pissed was an understatement. She and my dad would be the only ones to physically discipline us and they did that rather well.

Mom was so talented and had such a nasty temper that she could talk on the phone to her best friend, smoke a cigarette and chase us around the kitchen to wack us with a wooden spoon without getting burning ashes on the floor or missing a beat talking. Now, that's talent.

If we were being too loud, man the chase was on. She would spend hours gossiping on the phone about other nurses on her floor. I was 7 or 8 at the time.

My mom had a friend who hated kids. When she came over we would have to stay in our rooms. This friend in particular liked watching X-rated movies and we had to disappear. Classy! This is what a good mother does is allow people like this into the house and lock your kids in their rooms so you can watch porn. Super great! Mother of the year!

THE 80's

Mom was best friends with the woman who lived across the street. They did everything together and my sister played with their kids. However, those kids were so mean to me and my sister was really mean to me when they were around. I wanted nothing to do with them, however mom thought differently.

If they had a birthday party, I had to go. A sleepover, I had to go. I hated them as I didn't have a choice but to attend these things. Even to this day, I want nothing to do with them and I haven't seen them in years. They moved away when I was in third grade. Their moving to Iowa was the best thing EVER! Needless to say, I didn't miss them when they left. I don't hate them but I just don't have any need or want to have anything to do with them.

My mom would also make me hug family members or friends when I didn't want to. My mother took away my choices at a very young age. If she wanted me to go, she would make me go. My needs simply didn't and still to this day don't matter to her. Her friends, reputation and the dog matter more than I do or did.

Setting and maintaining boundaries was never taught to me. Thus, why people have been able to bully, manipulate, abuse, use and take advantage of me. My mother doesn't have or respect boundaries but simply demands that her needs be met over anyone else's.

Even today, when I try to set healthy boundaries, she becomes really mad. She gets super pissed and says whatever comes into her mind and spews mean, hateful things. Then after a few days everything is okay or at least she thinks it is.

She has no control over her emotions. She doesn't think about the consequences of her actions or how her actions affect other people, namely her family. Again, because nothing is ever her fault.

Consequently, at a young age, I learned to ignore my needs to meet her wants and needs. I never learned to care for my individual needs until much later in life.

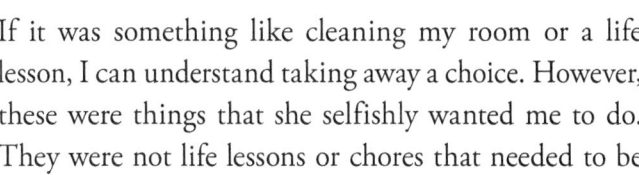

If it was something like cleaning my room or a life lesson, I can understand taking away a choice. However, these were things that she selfishly wanted me to do. They were not life lessons or chores that needed to be done. These were things that made her look good.

NEIGHBORHOOD DRAMA AND PURE HELL

In 1986, we had an incident with the nextdoor neighbors. Their youngest daughter and I were friends. She was 2 years younger than I. The previous night, my sister and I were playing with some other kids from the neighborhood in our backyard. The neighbor girl was ramming a stroller she brought over into the back of everyone's legs. My mom didn't say anything, but took note.

The kid got away with everything. She once stuck a fish hook she found in her yard into my back. I was so ashamed and I didn't want to tell my parents about it. My sister saw what happened and removed the hook from my back but there was still a puncture wound.

My sister forced me to tell them what happened. I was marched over to the next door neighbor's house and made to face the girl. She denied it but I had a puncture wound on my back. As per usual, nothing happened to her, but I had to get a tetanus shot.

The next morning, the neighbor girl wanted to play and brought the stroller. My mom told her she could come over and play, but she had to leave the stroller at home. Well, the girl told her mother that my mom had yelled at her or some such nonsense lie. She was well known for lying and being overdramatic.

This girl was so spoiled, entitled, and could do no wrong, that she could get away with murder. Well, her mom called mine and they ended up in a shouting match over the phone. Words were exchanged. My mom basically told her mom that if she wanted to "exchange names" to come over and say those things to her face.

Not the best thing to say to someone who has a seriously bad temper and flies off the handle in an instant. Actually, both women had bad tempers. Well, the neighbor showed up at the front door as asked and assaulted my mother. Cops were called.

Her husband was a police officer in the city we lived in and downplayed the whole incident. This would play over and over again in the following years. Assault charges were filed. When I came home from playing that afternoon my life changed dramatically.

My anxiety shot up so high and things were never the same. My childhood as I had known it ended that day. My world turned upside down and would never be the same again.

My mom simply told us that night that we were to avoid the neighbors. That I couldn't play with their daughter anymore and that we were to have no contact with them. Things went down from there.

This family was in the schools, they were revered in the city, county and were everywhere and involved in everything in the city.

We would receive hang-up calls routinely and daily after the incident. I think we would end up changing our phone number at least 20-30 times over the course of 10 years. The hang-ups were constant and came relentlessly regardless of whether we changed our phone number or not.

My mom and the mom who lived across the street would talk daily on the phone as they were the best of friends. We found out that their oldest daughter was simply giving our phone number to the neighbors without her mother knowing it. No matter how often we changed the number the hang-ups continued. The daughter was friends with the neighbor's middle daughter as they went to high school together.

Back then they had phone books and our number was unpublished. You could pay the phone company not to publish your phone number. Every time we changed the number, the oldest daughter across the street would simply give it to the neighbors' middle daughter. We were baffled as to how they would keep getting our number…until the daughter confessed.

The neighbors oldest son I'm pretty sure was Satan in the flesh. Much like his little sister, he could do no wrong. He and his family would terrorize me and my family for 10 years. I would fear walking home alone, I was humiliated in my own class, we were terrorized at home, I was bullied and left to hang on so many occasions.

Even families we knew well on our neighborhood block and were friends with, were afraid to stand up to this family. We would suffer alone while everyone sat and watched.

My mom wanted to move so desperately but my dad wouldn't have it. For some reason, she wanted to move into a trailer park? Why? I'm still not sure. My dad wouldn't budge on the subject. His house was his castle.

He would not move from that house come hell or high water. Mom became more and more depressed and desperate. The harassment was never-ending and the police just wouldn't do anything about it. After all, the husband was a cop, and a powerful one at that. We were basically left to defend ourselves.

For years, I was afraid to walk home alone from school. The neighbor girl would have her horrible friends surround me, call me a "Fat Bitch" and throw rocks at me. I was in second or third grade. At that time, I didn't even know what that word meant.

I was always sent to walk home with my sister or my mom picked me up after school. However, on some occasions, mom was working or my sister couldn't walk me home because she was going to sleep over at a friend's house or something like that.

The neighbor girl would leave me alone if I was with my sister. If I didn't have someone to walk home with this would cause a reign of terror in me. I didn't know how to defend myself (I hadn't been taught. I truly thought it was my fault.) and the humiliation and shame would engulf me for the whole day.

I would cry and cry. I was so scared and ashamed to go home alone. Why was this happening to me? Why would I or should I have had to endure this? I didn't do anything, yet this nightmare was my fault.

I would pray at night and cry myself to sleep begging to not have to go to school the next day. Oftentimes, the prayer was never answered. I would endure the bullying and it never ceased to end.

My really super great third grade teacher, because he had become so frustrated with me and my crying one day, marched me down to the second grade classroom where the youngest daughter from across the street was and put me with her so she could walk me home.

The humiliation, shame, embarrassment and pain were more than I could bear. It made me cry hysterically. I was so humiliated. My third grade teacher was truly horrible but not as truly horrible as my fifth grade teacher.

Maybe if my teacher had bothered to find out what was truly wrong or why I was crying maybe he would have understood. At that time, teachers didn't delve into those things. It was too much work.

Bullying wasn't seen as an issue that could cause life-long implications. It was just seen as something kids had to endure. It wasn't kids being kids, this was kids terrorizing kids. The school district did nothing and kept our neighbors in the schools regardless of our pleas to remove them from our school. It fell on deaf ears. They were reveared and we didn't matter. My pain and the humliation were sometimes more than I could bear.

They were monitors in the lunchroom, they were in the children's safety programming. Hell, they were everywhere. There was truly no one who would listen. I was afraid to buy milk in the cafeteria because they were in charge of selling it. I was only in the 3rd grade and afraid of them. 3RD GRADE! I would have terrible anxiety at lunch and basically couldn't eat anything and felt like I was going to be sick constantly.

I was having anxiety attacks, stomach aches and literally shaking uncontrollably. My parents tried for a reprieve. There wasn't one. Changing schools wasn't an option back then. They didn't have open enrollment. Where you lived decided what school you went to.

The School District simply didn't care that this family was terrorizing us in our own home and in school. The shame and pain it caused was never-ending. There was literally no escape for me. Somehow the most innocent of victims was the villain in this story.

Every now and then I would have kids come up to me in class and tell me that the neighbor girl told them that I was a bitch and so was my mom. This was in 3rd grade! The neighbor girl was in 1st grade. She truly was starting to learn those swear words young. She was the perfect little blessing…from Hell.

One day my mom, my sister and I were sitting outside in the front yard in the summer. For reasons still unknown to me, the neighbors oldest son floored their SUV up our 70 foot driveway and almost hit me and our dog. Had he not stopped he would have killed me and the dog instantly.

This was in broad daylight and other neighbors were outside as well. Finally, when he floored it back down the driveway and went home, my mom called the neighbor kitty corner from us who was also outside to see if she would back up our report.

She said she would as it was an attempted murder. Things had just gotten so bad between our households. Even to this day, I'm baffled as to why things just kept getting worse and worse. We weren't doing anything. They just became nastier and nastier. Finally, we had someone to corroborate our stories of harassment.

Previously, we would just be told it was our word against theirs and they would lie about what happened. Without witnesses to corroborate our story we didn't have a case. But this time, we finally had a witness who was actually friends with the neighbors who was willing to corroborate our story.

Amazingly, the next morning, the mother of the household wanted to bury the hatchet. For some reason, probably to end the never ending torment, my mom agreed. The mother knew her son would be charged and possibly jailed if we didn't agree.

That was the end of 10 years of a fight that started over a stroller. I never really could fathom and I still don't understand what could lead to such extreme hate. It's still a mystery to me now.

About 15-20 years later, the father was accused and served time for child molestation of his step-son. The son was the child of another relationship the mother had in high school. It had come out in the morning newspaper one day.

We always had suspicions of abuse but we thought it was the youngest daughter as she was so out of control. My mom told us at all costs to avoid any contact even after we had "buried the hatchet."

Strange things had been happening over there with people shouting at the house and the sheriffs office showing up daily knocking on the door. We had no idea and we weren't really good friends with them. It was more like we tolerated them and we didn't want to know.

The son had gotten himself into trouble for the billionth time and his step-father couldn't cover it up for him with law enforcement. Consequently, the charges showed up and the father was sent to prison for two or three years. I can't remember the exact amount of time.

Both daughters want nothing to do with either of their parents. They took out restraining orders to prevent either parent from having contact with their families. The mother chose to stand by her man. She still does. Whether this is the right thing to do, I'm not the judge. I know if it had been my child, my decision would have been much different.

Sadly, the son committed suicide a few years ago. He was not someone I ever cared to interact with. He was mean, a bully and he almost killed me with a vehicle. To be honest, there is no love lost.

Do I understand he was in pain…yes. However, there are many people who are in huge amounts of pain who don't go out of their way to make life hell for others just because they feel justified.

He had choices as we all do in our actions. He felt that he had a right to make our lives hell simply due to an incident that was blown way out of proportion from the beginning and based on a lie.

For this I feel justified in saying that when he faced his maker, I hoped he had to take a good, long look at his short life and what he did to us. My hope is that he felt remorse and found peace. I have forgiven and moved on but I will never ever forget the torment and hell he and his family caused me and my family.

Though now our households get along, it is still hard to swallow what happened. My sister wants nothing more to do with the family. I will talk to them and I have attended some events of theirs. I have gone to less and less as time goes on. The memories and events are a hard pill to swallow sometimes having gone through what we went through with them.

My sister is cordial but what happened, happened. It could have ended at any point. At any point the ridiculousness could have ended and it never had to escalate to attempted murder.

There was no reason it had to go on for so long or get so nasty. As adults, both women could have sat down and just had a respectful conversation. That's what adults do. However, neither my mom or the neighbor mom had the adult mental capacity to realize how ridiculous this feud was or that they both had the power at any time to end it.

10 years of torment, harassment and pain over a little girl's lie about a stroller. It's so asinine and such a waste to me even to this day.

LOVE AFFAIRS

My parents' marriage never seemed happy. My mom always wanted someone to take care of her or rescue her like a charming prince. My dad wanted nothing to do with that. He's not even close to that kind of guy. When we were young, he was more interested in hanging with his buddies and ignoring the needs of his wife and children.

That's not what marriage is about. It's about two people coming together with their faults, imperfections and love; making each other better by taking care of their own individual needs and bringing their best 'selves' to the partnership.

A couple knows that it will never be perfect but they love each other enough to say "let's keep going and I choose you." They work things out and fix things instead of giving the silent treatment or being passive aggressive, making excuses or avoiding the issue all together.

It's a give and take. My dad never realized that and still has no clue. It's still all about him. He still only takes and does not give, unless it is for my sister. My mom is the same way. It's all about her.

I don't think either of my parents learned what marriage was, and sadly they still have no idea. Consequently,

I would never know what a healthy marriage was or looked like. It would cost me dearly later in life.

My mom spent money like water flows. She always acted on impulse. If she wanted it, she got it. Consequences never seemed to be a thing mom thought about. She acted on impulse and still does to this day.

Anyway, she went looking in all the wrong places for love and acceptance. What she could never figure out is that both come from self-love, self acceptance and having self-worth which come from within not from outside.

In 1987, she would end up in the hospital on suicide watch. One night my dad just told my sister to watch me and that he and mom were going somewhere and would be back later. He had to take some time off work (I don't remember how much) just that he was home with us and took us to school, did the laundry and made meals. The usual things mom did. It was after 10:30pm that night when only dad came home. My sister and I were still up because why when you're in 3rd and 5th grade would you go to bed when there's no parent around?

The look in Dad's eyes almost brought me to my knees. Even in 3rd grade I could feel the pain and what they said broke my heart. "I"m dying." Dad died that night. He was never the same.

I became a "thing"; a "brat"; a "pest." He stayed for the 2 little humans who were 3rd and 5th grade. He laid down his life for them for the promise that his wife wouldn't hurt them.

It was a horrible trick. One most narcissistic parents like to pull. Ya see custody is usually given to the mother in Minnesota. He would lose his kids in court. So, he decided to bear it. However, he started hating the two little humans he was staying for.

This was different because dad always thought we should walk to school and not have mom take us. He was always angry about this. Another one of his "spoiled brat" things. Ya know, the" I had to walk uphill both ways in a blizzard" sort of thing." He actually took us to school while mom was in the hospital which was a huge shock.

Anyway, when mom came home after being in the hospital she pretty much stayed in their room crying. I liked to draw. I brought her a picture and gave it to her. She grabbed me and hugged me so tight and sobbed. Being the kid that I was, I just thought that somehow this was my fault.

I had never seen either of my parents cry and I felt so helpless. I wanted to make her feel better so I brought the drawing to her and somehow made it worse. Being that this never happened before, I just started crying, too. I didn't know what to make of this. I just wanted mom to feel better.

From that moment on I would be the one to try to keep my mother happy. Unbeknownst to me, this would be a never-ending, impossible task.

I wouldn't find out until some years later that she was having an affair with another man. The guilt and fear of being caught had led her to the hospital ward.

This, consequently, wouldn't be the last time or last affair. It would be the beginning of a trend in our family life. One that would play out over and over through my adolescent and teenage years.

That summer, we went to Montana on vacation to see if they could "rekindle" their relationship. We drove to Yellowstone park and saw the sites along the way. My sister and I would play in the back seat of our station wagon, not a care in the world. We even got to stay at Motel 6's on the way. They always kept the light on for us...

After about the 3rd or 4th Motel 6 mom told dad she wouldn't stay in another Motel 6 after we found something gross in the room we stayed at and that he'd BETTER find another hotel.

Needless to say, we got to stay in a really, really nice Holiday Inn in Spearfish, South Dakota. It was a kid's dream. 5 pools, waterslides. Gosh! My sister and I were in HEAVEN! That is until we arrived home.

Of course no vacation is complete without stopping at Wall Drug for some souvenirs AND a bumper sticker.

Dad would yell at us occasionally telling us to be quiet and threaten to pull over the car and leave us on the side of the road if we didn't be quiet. The empty threat would play out the whole vacation. It was as if the affair hadn't happened. However, when we arrived back from vacation the glaring truth was still there.

We never talked about that time or the numerous other times she would end up in the hospital on police lock up. We as a family just never talked about anything. The elephant in the room just sat there plain as day as if nothing was wrong.

It was a good vacation but things were never the same when we arrived home. Life would go on but their relationship was never and would never be the same ever again. Not that it was the happiest to begin with.

The dinner china had been broken. The pieces would never fit or look the same again. It would continue to be broken over and over until there were simply shards and there was nothing left to put back together. I did bring up the affairs and the drug addiction one time with my mother and told her that she caused me huge amounts of pain. To which she being the OUTSTANDING mother she is...said BIG DEAL!

APPETITE AND DESTRUCTION

I entered 4th grade weighing over 100 pounds. For some reason, I kept eating and eating or binging as I now know it. I believe this is when my binge eating disorder began. I also started going through puberty.

I started noticing things like hair growing in places it hadn't been before and I became so ashamed. I had to start wearing deodorant in 3rd grade. I was a size 18 in kids sizes and could only shop at Sears because they were the only place that had plus sizes for kids. This was also the time I started becoming more bullied at school.

When it came time for school shopping that summer before 5th grade I couldn't fit even into the largest women's sizes, an 18. The shame was enormous and so awful. I was sitting in the living room and I overheard my mom on the phone to what would be Jenny Craig asking if they would accept a ten-year-old into their program.

I cannot even describe the humiliation and shame of overhearing that phone call. I sobbed. My mom tried to comfort me by telling me that I was such a pretty girl and would be accepted if I would just lose some weight. As if her love depended on what size I was and what the scale said.

Because, evidently, I wasn't acceptable or lovable as I was. The message was loud and clear. I wasn't beautiful or acceptable unless I lost weight. If I put down the fork and ate less, all my problems would disappear. If only it were that easy. I felt SO unlovable and very, very ugly for SO long.

What many people don't understand is that obesity is partially about eating too much but it can also be a mental health issue. My anxiety about school made it so I couldn't eat breakfast in the morning. I would have such bad stomach aches worrying about the day ahead and what would or wouldn't happen.

I would be in school, and if the day was stressful, I would be too nervous to eat lunch so I binged emotionally when I got home from school. By that time I was starving. If I came home from school upset, I buried my pain in Doritos. If I was happy, it was a food reward. Emotionally eating became my go-to thing to feel better. Food became my refuge as I had few friends and it was an outlet for my anguish and shame.

Many times if I did eat my lunch, it was full of things like Hostess Twinkies and cupcakes, Fruit Roll Ups, Little Debbi treats or some other unhealthy things with a sandwich. Childhood obesity wasn't on anyone's radar back then.

I was binging because I was starving and, when I did eat my lunch, I ate junk, high calorie food. I knew no different. Heath class didn't exist back then until 5th grade and my parents just fed us what they thought we would eat. I just kept gaining more and more weight.

The threat of "you won't get a bedtime snack if you don't clean your plate" was also a common thing at my house. My parents were huge on cleaning your plate and finishing all the food even if you were already full.

Overeating and indulging was commonplace at my house. Dinner lasted about 7-10 minutes so I learned to inhale my food instead of eating mindfully and slowly. If food is eaten fast, it doesn't allow the body to feel full until overeating has occurred. This happened for years and years. I ate fast and I never gave my body a chance to feel completely full.

These ideas would be detrimental to my eating habits growing up along with the fact that my mom was constantly on a diet. She would eat so little, to fit into her Chic Jeans and curse her body in the mirror while my sister and I would watch her.

I remember looking in the mirror a few short years later and doing the exact same thing. I still struggle with body image and trying not to find fault with my body even today. What mom and dad never seemed to understand is that they had unhealthy eating habits and were passing them on to me. Even to this day my dad buys potato chips, cookies, donuts among other unhelathy snacks. He goes through a potato chip bag every day. No wonder he's having health issues.

My parents would eat breakfast and then not eat until dinner. Both my parents would eat a tiny bit at dinner and eat sweets the rest of the night. This is the trend I saw growing up. I knew no different at the time or how truly unhealthy it was.

My dad exercises like a mad man at the gym. He turns the elliptical up to the highest level and works out for an hour. His body is now so used to it that he's starting to get a gut. The man eats sweets and potato chips like there is no tomorrow.

He looks healthy and fit but his diet is extremely unhealthy. To be healthy and fit, it matters what is eaten. He's never understood this fact. One can exercise for hours, but if high caloric food is eaten instead of healthy food, weight gain happens. This is what is happening to my dad.

My mom still tries to lose weight by measuring everything she eats, which is the wrong way to diet. She will eat very little at dinner and eat sweets all night so it's no wonder why she has gained so much weight.

My dad has blood pressure issues and my mom is very close to being a type II diabetic. Both believe that if you exercise enough, what you eat doesn't matter. Truth is, it does matter more than whether you exercise. I've learned that the hard way.

I've finally overcome the issues I had with eating, thankfully. I never knew how much or what to eat. I know that unhealthy food is not good for you but that is all my mother made for us when we were young.

Hotdishes or casseroles, hamburgers, McDonalds for a treat or a pizza. All are chocked full of fat and that is what we ate daily. If we had vegetables they had large amounts of butter and salt poured on them.

Consequently, my sister would be the only one who figured out how to eat healthy. I didn't figure this out for a very long time. She would ultimately be the one who would be one of my biggest health and finance champions much later in life. Really, those were the only things she ever supported me on, sadly.

I remember I had to follow my diet for a health project in school which is a common project in health class. I wrote down everything I ate in a week or two weeks. My health teacher didn't believe that I had done the project and gave me a "C" saying basically that no one could eat the way I described.

He was convinced that I hadn't done the project and made it up at the last minute which wasn't true. I was shocked at the grade as I had always done well in Health class (grade-wise and a teacher had never accused me of making something up or not doing my work until that time).

It was the first, small indication that maybe something was wrong? However, no one heeded the warning and I just thought it was normal.

The start of fifth grade wasn't anything special. I was over 110 pounds and there were no red flags being waived. My mom simply thought that since she was big as a child that it was hereditary or something.

No doctor visits to address the problem or see that there was an issue. Doctor visits were extremely expensive because my dad's employer had high-deductible insurance at the time.

I remember having a bad ear infection one time and my mom couldn't get me in to see the pediatrician until later in the week. My mom constantly asked me if my ear still hurt and I told her it did. I was just in Kindergarten or first grade. I didn't know any better. Anyway, when we went for the appointment the doctor asked me where it hurt and I told him it didn't hurt anymore.

He looked in my ears and the infection was gone. My mom was pissed that I didn't tell her so she could cancel the appointment. They would have to pay for the appointment. She ostracized me.

This would be an ongoing thing in my life. I was devastated when this happened. My mom knew she had power over me and would use it relentlessly against me growing up. She had a "death stare" like no one I've ever seen. It scared the shit out of me when I was young.

I actually inherited it along with my naturally curly hair. The only two good things I inherited as I use the "death stare" when I'm putting someone in "their place" at the pharmacy or elsewhere. It totally shuts people up.

I also just really love my hair. Again, the only two good things from her.

In school, the truth was, I was binging more and more. I had few, if any, friends and I was withdrawing more and more. I was also tormented at school. When I was in my room, I would hide in my closet and simply sob uncontrollably. The shame, hurt and pain were so overwhelming. Consequently, no one ever found me or knew that I was in so much pain.

I hated my life at that time and had written in my diary that I wanted to die. My mom found it and sat me down to tell me how "concerned" it made her. Though she was not concerned enough to get me help. The bullying was so bad that I was having stomach aches where I simply couldn't eat without feeling that I had to throw up. I wouldn't, but the anxiety was horrible.

I finally found a way to end my torment by telling my mom that my stomach was upset and that it felt like I was going to be sick almost every morning. I got away with this for a while. I had missed a lot of school but she eventually asked me what was going on and why I didn't want to go to school.

I was so full of shame but I told her that I was being bullied and which of the boys was doing it. She went to school with me the next day and told my teacher who was well aware of what was going on but didn't say anything.

This would make things worse, not better. My teacher just didn't want to deal with it and hated me in the first place. He continued to hand out a "slap on the wrist" for the boys and they continued tormenting. The only difference was that I had no way out. School was my hell and suffering was something I became accustomed to, unfortunately.

GRANDMA: MY SAVIOR AND GRACE

The one person in my life that I could count on and who seemed to understand me was my paternal Grandmother. She seemed to understand things about me that no one else seemed to know. Not even me.

She was able to love me despite my weight, sensitivity and accept me wholly for who I was. I didn't need to be "thin" and I wasn't a "brat" or a "pest" to her. She loved me for the child that I was at the time.

When my younger cousin's or sister were mean to me, she would do something about it. I loved my Grandmother so much that losing her was such an emotional, mental and physical blow to me.

She was a type II diabetic, a pack-a-day smoker, simply loved sweets and like many Americans, hated exercise. She had been in the hospital a few different times related to heart issues. The fourth one would be her last.

I always worried about losing her, but for some reason the last time, I truly thought she would make it through. Consequently, she didn't. I was devastated. I felt like I lost more than just a Grandparent, she was my mom on so many levels. The only one I truly had. The loss was like losing a part of myself and my soul.

Grandma was a woman who loved God and her family fiercely. She loved Christmas and the church. She would try to instill those values into her children...well...for the most part.

Grandma was always upset that my sister and I never went to Sunday School and often feared for our Christian education into the Lutheran Church. My parents had priorities like sleeping in on Sundays doing whatever they wanted except going to church like Grandma wanted.

I mean, we went to church on holidays like Christmas and Easter which my parents thought was enough. Mom didn't like church, it reminded her of the death of her mother or some such nonsense like that.

She is probably the one that never wanted to go, knowing her, but I can't remember for certain. All that I know is that we were "holiday church-goers" until my sister hit 8th grade for confirmation.

It was a Saturday morning when the phone rang and my parents were told to come to the hospital. Grandma had been brought in a few days before as she had collapsed in the apartment she and my grandfather shared. My mom asked her older sister, our Aunt, to come and get my sister and I and to take us to her house.

It didn't seem like a day for death, but I knew nothing of death or what it should've looked like at that time. No one I knew had died before. I had a keen sense that people don't come back but it became quite real when mom said Grandma passed away.

I really couldn't figure out why it wasn't raining or storming as I was so angry, sad and confused. I had lost the one person who actually understood me.

How much I wanted the sky to open up and storm a storm like it had never stormed before because it felt that way in my soul. I wanted to scream, cry, yell, but it was no use. Nothing was going to bring her back. She was gone…forever.

I wanted to hold someone responsible…God…whoever. I just wanted my Grandma back. Really, they could have whatever they wanted that the fifth grader that I was, owned. Honestly. "Just please bring my Grandma back" was all I could think about or wanted at that time.

I couldn't believe I didn't get to see her. I didn't get to say goodbye or say "see you later." That I would never get to hug her or tell her that I loved her. That we would never play board games anymore.

Grandma could play a mean game of Trouble and/or Hearts. She was one helluva woman and I would have a gaping hole in my life without her. She passed away on April 29 1989, nine days before my 12th birthday.

For the funeral, my sister and I still went to school the day of Grandma's wake. It added insult to injury, the boys in my 5th grade class were intensely cruel that day. I don't remember all the specifics, but one boy was the worst. He simply was cruel beyond cruel. His harassment was never ending. That day, all I wanted to do was escape, disappear, or simply vanish into thin air and not come back.

This boy and his gangly gang of simpletons simply wouldn't leave me alone. One of the girls in my class told my horrible 5th grade teacher that the boy was being mean to me during recess.

My teacher marched me over to the boy and made him apologize but not before chastising me for "causing problems." After the boy apologized, he showed me his "crossed fingers" which in kid language means "not."… "not sorry," "not anything"… "takebacks."

It was the millionth dagger in an already dying or close to dead heart. I had lost the one person who not only believed in me, who would fight fire for me and love me no matter what. I lost the only real mother I would ever have. To say I was crushed is a true understatement.

Often I would feel so empty throughout my adolescent and teenage years. Even in my 20's I felt this gaping hole in my "self." I always attributed it to the loss of my Grandmother. It was part of it but part of it was I was so "empty" inside. I don't know when it truly developed but it was the beginning of my Borderline Personality Disorder. I would try to fill it with shopping and buying needless things from Target or any other store where I would waste money on things I didn't need or even want in an attempt to feel whole. It never worked. The hole was always there and wouldn't be filled in until later in my life.

Though it was a loss of quantifying Grandma's death would have life-long lasting implications for me on so many levels of my life. I still miss her to this day. She meant so much to me.

Many days I would spend thinking about why her loss was so great. After all, kids lose their Grandparents first, usually. I never knew my mothers' parents. They both died before I was born. I've come to the conclusion that if Grandma had lived, I would not have gone through the traumas I endured in my life.

Those traumas have made me the person I am today. My trauma has helped me to understand people better, to be able to walk in their shoes, read and feel their vibe energy and know what to say to add comfort to lessen pain. My Love Languages are "Words of Affirmation" and "Gift Giving." I hate seeing people in pain; emotionally, physically or mentally because I have endured so much of it.

I wouldn't be as strong mentally, emotionally or physically had she lived. She would have fought all my battles for me. I would have simply hid behind her not getting to experience pain, shame, fear, humiliation, heartbreak or failure which are a huge part of life. What I didn't learn is that it didn't and shouldn't of had to be a main factor in my life like it was growing up.

I needed to experience those things to be who and what I am. I am also an Empath. These "gifts" have enabled me to help others' in so many positive ways. Because of my experiences, I'm able to walk in another person's shoes. To feel their pain and empathize with them on another level with their situations.

WOMANLY THINGS

I had started going through puberty when I was in 3rd grade. My breasts started developing and I was really, really ashamed. One day, in 4th grade I was in line and a friend of mine ran a pencil eraser down my back catching my bra and snapping it. The whole class heard it and I was mortified enough to stop wearing a bra.

I would be so ashamed of the changes in my body as no one told me I would be growing hair in certain areas, or about the changes that would take place. Sex education was a hot topic back then and the religious prudes of the community didn't think it should be taught in school.

The school district was engulfed in a tug-of-war between those that thought that sex ed should be left to the parents and those that thought that it should be taught in schools. Consequently, I received no direction or information on the changes that would take place that year. I was terrified, unprepared and ashamed when they did come.

Nothing compared to the shame I felt when my menstrual cycle arrived. One day we were out to breakfast and when we came home my mom told me to go to the bathroom and to look in my underwear. For what, I didn't know. I was terrified when I found blood in my underwear.

She came in and gave me a pad and told me something like "welcome to womanhood." She didn't really discuss it. It wasn't happiness at becoming a woman or informational it was: this is going to go on for most of your life so here's a pad. Happy trials. I cried as my lacking childhood had ended and womanhood at a very young age had arrived, so incredibly uninvited.

Because of my experience with parents who never discussed the changes that would happen later in my childhood years, I'm an advocate for teaching sex ed in the schools. I'm also an advocate of having condoms and birth control pills in schools. With the controversy surrounding Planned Parenthood and states banning abortion, education in the classroom is needed now more than ever.

Kids are experimenting with sex more than they did when I was in school. I don't believe that having contraception in K-12 schools promotes sex. It prevents unwanted pregnancies and STI transmission.

The prude religious population needs to wake up and realize that promoting abstinence is not working. Having young women make pledges to wait until they are married to have sex is not only sexist but also unrealistic with what kids see today in the media, movies and on TV.

Giving teens the tools to protect themselves from unwanted pregnancies and sexually transmitted infections does work and saves them from a lifetime of poverty. Unplanned pregnancies in the teenage years can prevent young women from going to college and higher paying jobs.

The responsibilities of having a baby at that young age are too much, especially since teens can be impulsive and the human brain isn't usually 100 percent developed until age 25. It's a very adult decision to start having sex but one mistake, lacking education and lack of available protection should not lead to a lifetime of poverty.

For my sex education in 10th grade, we had a religious couple come and discuss their reason for waiting until marriage to have sex and how it had somehow strengthened their relationship. I don't believe it stopped anyone in class from having sex. For all I know, the couple could be divorced by now and their "special" bond for waiting until they were married could be broken and yesterday's news.

I was too disgusted with my body to have sex and I actually bought into the whole waiting until I was married to have sex. I didn't marry until I was 38 and I started having sex when I was 32. I was so inexperienced and clueless that it wasn't even something I enjoyed doing.

It actually hurt and I simply didn't see what all the fuss was about. I paired love with sex and they are two separate things. They can and should be together with the right person but I chose all the wrong ones. This would be a very painful lesson later in life.

6TH GRADE

Life went on and stayed the same for all of 6th and 7th Grade. I was still tormented but the boy that did most of the bullying was in a different class. My 6th grade teacher hated our class. For some reason, some kids simply wouldn't listen.

My teacher would give and take away points for a popcorn party or recess. Consequently, we were such a bad class that we sometimes missed recess altogether and never earned enough points for a popcorn party.

There was a kid in my class who was just different. He would always end up sitting at the front of the classroom in the corner as my teacher would get really frustrated with him and put him there as a punishment. Most of the kids in class would tease and torment him.

His family was financially strapped. He really annoyed me so I would be mean to him as well. I regret this now. Now, I realize that there was probably something wrong mentally or physically with him. Disabilities in kids wasn't a thing they took seriously back then.

One afternoon, my teacher became so frustrated with the kid that he took the kids' desk and dumped it on the ground and made the boy pick up the mess. The whole class, including me, thought it was hilarious. The poor kid was humiliated and no one in the class, I'm ashamed to say, stuck up for him.

It was a lesson in cruelty that he has probably never forgotten. Defining moments in time where I wish I could go back and change so it would have a different outcome. I have many such moments in my life looking back. If I could apologize to let him know how truly sorry I am, I would.

My teacher sat there and humiliated this child who simply had a mental or physical disability in front of the whole class. I look back now and realize how awful that must have felt. How alone and ashamed he must have been. It must have been gut-wrenching to say the least. A defining moment in time.

Our class was the last 6th grade class the elementary school had as they were changing the grades from K-5 in elementary, 6-8 in the junior high/middle school and 9-12 at the high school. They decided to make this change to my class.

In 6th grade, we were required to take swimming lessons as part of the physical education curriculum. I hated swimming class as all the 6th grade classes were put together and my bully would torment me while I was in class.

I looked awful in my bathing suit as it was a women's size 18 and I simply wasn't grown into the chest quite yet so the straps would always fall down. I also could never dive correctly, always doing belly flops to the amusement of my peers.

The days I got to miss swimming were a Godsend. I was allowed to stay in the classroom and do whatever I wanted. It was great. I hated swimming more than anything else.

My graduation from sixth grade was uneventful. My teacher still blamed me for the torment I received and said I had to be "less sensitive" in what was then junior high. Again, blaming me for the horrible behavior of the boy's in my grade.

I would enter 7th grade clueless, friendless and alone but I wasn't tormented, teased or bullied. Thankfully, I was left alone for the most part.

8TH GRADE CRUSHES AND THE "SUMMER" OF "SOMEONE IS WATCHING"

I would leave 6th grade and go onto junior high. Though the bullying had stopped since I left elementary school. Most of the kids in my elementary school went to a different junior high or middle school.

Since I was "Too" sensitive, too "this" too "that" I learned to be a new person. Being that I wasn't' accepted for who I was, I changed into a person that I thought people would accept. I had learned to be a more pleasing and a totally new fake me would emerge.

A totally fake person I would learn to despise. I hated her SO much! I would bury the person I was, too ashamed of who I really was to let the real me show. The "fake" me was perfect in every way, she was the good girl, the pleasing girl, the one who smiled through it all, the funny "dumb" one.

The one who never misbehaved or "rocked the boat," the one who "behaved." If I've learned anything from other women, a well behaved woman gets stomped on, used and or possibly killed. The woman who steps out of line saves her own life and goes on to save and advocate for others.

I watched a story on TED Talk about one woman's grandmother who in WWII was lined up next to the pits where they were simply shooting jewish people in the back. Her grandmother asked a Nazi what would happen if she stepped out of line. The Nazi didn't have an answer so she stepped out of line and was saved.

Women who have the courage to step out of line have helped future generations step forward in society. I will never stand in line again.

Good girls get used! Get out of line and mess shit up, see where you can go, don't EVER be pleasing. Brave women make societal waves and change lives for the better. Rock the fucking boat and tip the fucking thing over, create thunder, storms, hurricanes, and typhoons to make change happen. Just whatever you do, don't stay in line! As that womans' grandmother learned, it could cost you your life.

The new me wouldn't get stellar grades but people thought she was smart and funny and "dumb." Striving wasn't something I did. I could have pulled A's had I been believed in or thought that it was worth it. If I had been encouraged or even thought that I was smart.

I wasn't ever "enough." I wasn't smart enough, good enough or seem to matter. I was just "there." I simply existed.

C's just seemed acceptable and my parents were satisfied with that from me. They never pushed or believed I could do better. My sister, however, was a different story. She was encouraged and pushed to get A's and B's. If teachers didn't give my sister the grades my mother thought she deserved, she would argue and rip the teacher a new asshole.

One such teacher I would end up having in 7th grade wouldn't give my sister an A so mom ripped him a new one.

I ended up having him for 7th and 8th grade social studies. No matter how hard I worked, even in group work, he would only give me C's. I worked really hard in his class. This would not be the first or last time I would pay for my mother's wrath against teachers who didn't give my sister the grades mom thought she deserved.

However, when it came to me, mom would just accept what the teacher gave me for a grade. The attitude was "this is the best Melissa can do." Sadly, I never learned to strive, felt I could do better or ever supported and believed in.

I would hit my growth spurt and thin out a bit. I was a size 16 in 7th grade and down to a womens 10 in 8th. Not bad, but I also tried starving myself, eating only 3 tiny things a day.

It didn't last long as I almost fainted one day, so I stopped. I still put myself on a diet and I was quite strict on what I was eating. It seemed to please my mom as I was losing weight which seemed to make her happy.

If I had to choose a grade where I was ecstatically happy, it would be the 8th grade. I had finally broken through my shyness, I was thinner, I had real, fake friends and I wasn't being bullied. I had my first crush and I was so happy. That is, until Valentine's Day of 1992.

I had this really sad way of asking boys out that I would write a note and give them my phone number. I was waaay too shy to even ask them face-to-face. The fear of rejection was so overpowering and crippling that I just didn't have it in me to ask anyone out or take the chance of rejection.

Anyway, I had given a note to my secret crush. That Friday I had a sleepover with a friend. We for some reason had his phone number and called his house. His dad answered and said he wasn't home. I didn't leave my name but had high hopes for some reason that he would call. Sadly, he never did. I would be crushed but not before Valentine's Day.

Valentine's Day came and I was so positive in my adolescent mind that he would bring me flowers. Why? I still don't know. I remember seeing him come through what were called the "South" doors in school that day and he had a balloon and flowers.

I was ready to talk to him when he walked right straight past me and gave them to his former girlfriend who he had asked out again the Friday before, unbeknownst to me. Gah!

The punch in the gut was just the icing on the cake. The fact that the asshole put on a show was like taking a golf cleat and stomping on my young heart ten billion times. As a result, I vowed to hate Valentine's Day for the rest of my days.

February is still my least favorite month partially due to the weather and also Valentine's Day which is a just a hard day for me as I've never had anyone who was "special" to celebrate it with me. My ex never chose to do anything with me on Valentine's Day. I still hate Valentine's Day to this day. It's simply a Hallmark holiday. I've never had a guy that did anything positive for me or actually "loved" me in a way I understood. The Hallmark Holiday is one of my least favorite days. Valentine's Day in elementary school was hell. I often received few valentines before they made the rule that each kid in the class had to receive on. The day would cause anxiety for me. Kids are really nice to the kid that's shy and "different" after all.

The day is upon us and I just have so many bad memories of it.

The day is simply a joke to me. This heart-wrenching incident would not be the last time my heart would be broken but it would be one of the most memorable and the one that caused the first real "heartbreak" in my life.

I was set to go to a different high school than the rest of my friends. I so wanted to go to the school that my friends were going to. I would have given anything for it. It was devastating to me to lose my best fake friends I had worked so hard to find.

However, the district, due to a stupid boundary decision, sent me and about 20 other kids from my class to a school half-way across the city where we knew no one. This would prove to be quite detrimental to me mentally and emotionally.

I would finish 8th grade and move into summer vacation. My sister would start working at Denny's as a dishwasher. My mother would become paranoid, be on medical leave from work due to a "mystery illness;" and my dad would work so much overtime to keep the bills paid that we barely saw him. Oh, and we would go to Disneyland with my Aunt, Uncle and Cousin.

As 8th grade ended, I remember walking out of school with a good friend of mine and telling her that I would see her soon. She was also in my confirmation class at church as were many of the kids who I went to school with. It didn't seem like goodbye. I just assumed summer was here and didn't have a concern in the world. Except that this would be the summer from Hell at home.

Mom had to get vaccinated as a nurse working with the public so having her take the hepatitis vaccine when it came out was not something that anyone thought would cause problems in any way.

She had gotten the vaccination but became very ill from it. She had a very bad reaction to the yeast in the shot and this would unleash anger, paranoia, resentment and threats of retaliation against her employer at the expense of her family, friends and strangers we encountered.

After getting sick, mom would be weak and almost like a yellowly color. She was actually sick most of that summer but her mental state is what concerned and frightened us the most. Mom went to the hospital and found out that the department where she had been given a vaccine vial that had been left out of the refrigerator. The vaccine is one that always needed to be in a temperature controlled environment. Leaving it out of the fridge caused the yeast in the vaccine to multiply. Mom is allergic to yeast and she became very ill.

Her allergy to yeast is what made her so ill. She wanted to sue. Man, to say she was pissed doesn't even begin to scratch the surface of her rage. To say she hated her employer was an understatement. However, because she could sue didn't mean she had witnesses to corroborate her story.

She did visit several lawyers all armed with hearsay but did not have anyone to corroborate her story. Consequently, the lawyers all told her the same thing; that she didn't have a case without evidence or someone to corroborate her story.

She took this as her employer retaliating against her. The doctors, lawyers, nurses, janitors, housekeepers and security officers of the hospital were all "against" her. They were in a plot to destroy her good name. As if she wasn't doing a good job of this herself, already.

She would "hear" things, voices, or believe the house was "bugged" or the car was "bugged" or that people, family members and friends we knew were "in on it."

What "it" was and why she thought this way was never really explained. She would leave us in the car for hours to talk to clerks at convenience stores regarding the "plot" her employer was taking against her.

My sister, my dad and I were victims in a never ending saga. My mother had to get back at her employer at any expense for ruining her health and interfering in her life and family.

Mom refused to work and she had also written over $20,000 worth of bank checks on the line of credit against the mortgage. Ya know those checks the bank used to give to mortage holders that you can add to your mortgage credit line . The banks gave blank checks for this. Unfortunately, mom found them as dad had hidden them from her. It was PAYDAY for mom.

Mom found the checks and wrote out $5000.00 at a time totaling over $20,000. My dad, when he found out about it, saying he was PISSED is like saying Mount Everest is only a tiny hill.

Not only had she added years onto the mortgage he was working extremely hard to pay it off early; she didn't have an explanation of where exactly the money went or what she bought. I have a strong suspicion that it went to one of the men she was having another affair with at the time.

These are the "affairs" that we "know" of. I'm guessing there were others that we simply don't know about. There was nothing to show for that amount of money being spent. Consequently, he had to pick up every shift of overtime possible to keep us housed.

Since mom would only sit, smoke cigarettes all day and pet the dog. We had no groceries for weeks on end. She was on "Family Medical Leave" or overall medical leave and wasn't working. Essentials like toilet paper, food and dog food for the dog were not being bought.

Dad had to pay the mortgage and afford the general bills like electric, water and the garbage bill. Food was something that mom bought but she was on one of many medical leaves that would happen and simply didn't care that we needed to eat.

Mom was responsible for buying groceries. She couldn't be trusted to pay the other bills but groceries and her credit cards were her only responsibility. She epically failed as she would go weeks without buying any food thus causing me to binge when food was available.

Most of the time food wasn't available. It was like a feast and famine at our house. However, mom did have a pack-a-day smoking habit which was surprisingly sustained during that time. Everyone has their priorities, I guess. Consequently, her own children were not one of them.

I wasn't old enough to work, but I had been given an allowance that I was saving. My sister came to me and said I had to take my allowance and she would take her paycheck from her job and we would buy groceries as we were so hungry.

So, a 14-year-old and a 16-year-old went grocery shopping for food we could eat and make ourselves.

Our selection was quite limited to convenience food but at least we could eat it because it wasn't like mom was going to cook anything. Priorities, after all. There was a dog that needed babying and cigarettes that needed to be smoked. God forbid that the tobacco companies not get their money from my mother. Fuck the kids was basically her overall attitude.

We knew nothing about food shelves and my parents probably wouldn't have accepted the help due to their pride. We came home from grocery shopping to find my mother again, sitting and petting the dog looking at us like "screw you brats." "See mommy doesn't care," and the pain she caused on so many, many levels wouldn't end that summer. It was just the start of this type of bizarre behavior.

I would get to go on two vacations that summer. My cousin was moving down to Missori to live with her husband-to-be. They wanted someone to ride with her down there so she wasn't driving alone. I would spend 4 days there. It was a nice reprieve from my mother.

However, when I got back, it was worse. My mom had asked if I want to go to the local mall and look around. On the way there, I said something that she deemed "suspicious" about where we were going and she totally flipped out.

She accused me of being "in on it." I thought she was going to do something horrible to me. She was hysterical. At that point, I just wanted to go home. For the first time in my life, I feared my mother and what she would do to me.

I prayed all the way back home that she wouldn't do something horrible to me. She did drive us home but not after berating me for my "suspicious" comment. She wouldn't talk to me for a couple of days which was fine with me. As time went on, things just got worse and worse.

Even though things were extremely tight money-wise, we did manage to take a vacation to Disneyland that year. My aunt and uncle lived in Arizona. We flew down there and we drove over to California with them. My sister and I were given a short reprieve from the hell our mother was causing.

My sister and I hung out with our cousin who would provide a great escape. He was two years older than my sister and funnier than hell. We were allowed to go off with him at Disneyland which was a Godsend. Escaping my mother and the pure hell she was causing was truly a huge blessing at that time.

My Dad, Aunt and Uncle corralled my mother at the park. Unfortunately, she saw some woman she knew who worked on a different floor at the hospital at the park and all hell broke loose.

The conspiracy theories just flew right out of her mouth. She started accusing my aunt and uncle of being "in on it" because they kept telling her she was paranoid. That just made her more and more agitated and angry. My dad had to step in and calm her down which was no easy feat at that time.

She wanted to go right to the airport right then and there and fly the hell out of there. If the woman could fly she had the rage of a learjet flying at top speed on a suicide mission to divebomb her employer who she felt had wronged her on so many levels.

We would go to restaurants and if someone said anything she deemed "suspicious," she would accuse them of being "in on it." It was like a mini witch hunt. I still don't know what "it" was. I wish I knew what the hell "it" was. All the pain, humiliation and shame "it" caused and to this day, and I still don't have any idea what the hell "it" was.

We stopped going to restaurants or tried to eat at home as much as possible. This was difficult as there was

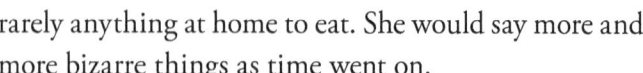

rarely anything at home to eat. She would say more and more bizarre things as time went on.

THE HELL OF THE SUMMER WOULD MERGE WITH THE HELL OF STARTING HIGH SCHOOL

For high school, I was separated from many of my fake friends who went to another school. I was forced to go to a school halfway across the city due to a school border. I fought like hell to go to the school my friends went to but the school district wouldn't let me attend the school of my choice due to overcrowding. I would spend the year severely depressed.

One night my mom was on the phone and she received a call for me. We had call waiting where you could accept two calls on the home phone. Old, yes, I know. She gave the phone to me and the person on the other end threatened to kill me in various unpleasant ways for talking about someone named "Kelly." Now, I had no idea who the hell "Kelly" was, much less, and I had not talked about her or anyone else in school that day.

I was scared shitless. My mom told me I didn't have to go to school the next day. However, I knew that if I didn't go, the bully would win. Nowadays, the school would press charges and do precautionary things. Back then it was unheard of to do those things.

I went to school the next day scared to death. Thankfully, nothing happened but that was definitely a defining moment in my high school career. I hated the school and the people for the rest of the year. I missed my junior high fake friends and only wanted to go to the school where they were. It would define my 9th grade year.

Thankfully 10th grade was much better than my 9th grade year. I finally found some friends but they were from all different groups. I didn't have my own "tribe." I would be a misfit throughout high school and throughout my adult life. I never really fit in anywhere and I knew I was "different" somehow.

I didn't enjoy being out doing the things high schoolers like doing. I was more of a homebody and somewhat of a nobody. I really wasn't excited to learn how to drive or have independence. I was more afraid of it than anything.

Becoming an adult scared the shit out of me even though I'd been acting older than I was with the responsibilities of an adult for quite some time. I didn't feel I was ready to "legally" be an adult. I was still that lost child and would be for quite some time.

My 10th and 11th grade years would be about the same. Nothing too exciting. I would join choir in 11th grade with a good friend and my teacher would accuse me of joining choir to get into a social group which wasn't true. My mom would yell at my teacher at conferences and he would make me pay for it.

This was a constant scene at conferences when my mom attended. She insisted on telling my teachers what she thought of them and their teaching. I would end up paying the price. I absolutely hated it when my mom attended my conferences. She would also do this to my sister's teachers but it didn't seem like my sister was blamed like I was.

I joined the choir because I wanted to. I had a good friend who had been in choir the year before and she convinced me to join. I would end up in a threesome friendship where I was squeezed out. I ended up hating choir because of one other person who my friend became friends with. She basically drove us apart. They say 3's a crowd and that is very true.

I would lose my friend that year and it was devastating. Though we would make up in 12th grade, the damage had been done at the time. I would become so tired of the third person coming into my friendships which would be defining factors in my relationships in my teens and 20's. I came to despise anyone who tried to come into my friendships not knowing that this was a truly normal thing in life.

People are in your life either as a blessing or a lesson they say. Many came into my life as a lesson. I would learn and relearn that lesson over and over again until I passed that life chapter.

I hated high school so much that I went on the internship program in 12th grade because I couldn't stand being in school a full day anymore. I just didn't want to be babysat anymore.

I would go to work for a carpet wholesaler as a file clerk. I would have a Monday-Friday job but home would be a mess again. Mom was again having paranoia issues, and as per usual, Dad did nothing. It was my senior year and she was in and out of the hospital on police lock-up.

Yet again, she admitted she had an affair with someone she met at Hardees. She would go there after dropping me off at school and spend time with the regulars there. She met this dirty, disgusting guy who "made her feel special." No other sane, respectful woman would ever touch the guy with a 10 foot pole he was so gross. She would yet again, blow our family life apart.

I hated the men she had affairs with. They destroyed my family. However, I now realize that she is just as guilty. She made the choice to cheat. I could never be a "homewrecker." I could never rip a family apart. That's not who I am and I respect myself too much to ever be the "other woman." I won't play second in my relationships when I deserve to play first.

I also cannot be the cause of that kind of pain for another woman. It's truly agony. The pain is enduring and lasts quite a while. I will never be the cause of that kind of pain. I've been on the other side of affairs and the anger, resentment and broken trust truly is a horrible experience.

After all that, dad still didn't divorce her. Again, he didn't want to uproot our lives. Thing is, I wouldn't have cared. I hated my mother so much for this. Having her gone would have been a huge blessing. Watching my dad fall apart and hurt again was more than I could bear. The pain it caused was unbearable.

I became my dad's confidant. Again, I was an adult before my time. One day we were talking and he told me to never ever cheat on my spouse. That if I was unhappy, to just get a divorce. He said the betrayal was the worst pain one can ever endure.

I would take that advice to heart later in life. From then on, I made a promise to myself that I would never do that to someone I loved. If I was unhappy in my marriage, I would divorce and not cause that kind of pain. It was agony seeing my father that way.

I swore from that moment on, I would never cheat. NEVER! The pain of what she had done to our family twice now or more was enduring and the betrayal was sometimes more than I could handle. It was also my senior year of high school. One of the most important years of my life, and now the focus was on her, yet again.

Nevermind, that she had wanted to leave with the guy. I wished she had and that would be a defining fact that would change the face of my relationship with my mother for life. I never fully trusted, believed in her or much less wanted the same relationship with her as I had before.

For some seniors in my class, their mother was their cheerleader, best friend and biggest supporter. My mother was my worst nightmare and the cause of agonizing pain and everything that was wrong or went wrong in our family.

Mom never would and still does not understand that her actions had and do have consequences. This was totally all about her and no one else mattered. She is still like this but just older.

She acts purely on her selfish wants and needs like a child. She simply did and does what "feels" good regardless of the consequences. It has never occurred to her that other people have feelings and that her actions have an effect on others, namely her family. However, we didn't and still don't matter even to this day. Unfortunately mostly me, my dad and sister are an afterthought. It was mostly my milestones she ruined for some reason. My achievements and things that were achievements in my young life were always somehow always about her or she played center stage.

I would seek out other women to fulfill her role. Sometimes I was successful for a time. Again, people come into your life when you need them most. I truly am grateful for the women who stepped up.

I will be forever grateful. I never told my friends at school what was going on at home. I was too ashamed and embarassed. I honestly don't remember for how long but I do remember she was so paranoid that she entered the hospital under my sister's first name and her maiden last name. This caused huge problems with the health insurance company as my dad had to literally beg them to cover the expensive hospital costs. Why she entered under a false name is still a mystery to me even to this day.

For Christmas the following year, mom was buying my sister and I gifts upon gifts as make-up for what she had done. Most of the gifts we didn't want, need or even use. Somehow this did not make anything better or change my relationship with my mother. I still wanted nothing to do with her. I remember my sister saying how "used" and "bought" she felt.

Consequently, I felt the exact same way. Dad was spending more and more time at work and I was wishing I could live at my employer. I hated Fridays. I remember crying at work when no one was around because I had to go home at the end of the day as I had no where else to go.

Home was not a place I wanted to be. This would be how things would go. In fact, this is how many special occasions, and holidays would go for a very long time. The focus would be on mom and her mental health issues, controlling the humiliation, shame and damage she caused us. It became exhausting trying to make

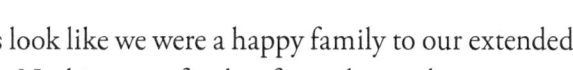

things look like we were a happy family to our extended family. Nothing was further from the truth.

At my aunts for Christmas that year, she freaked out. My uncle's brother was in and out of jail and just had a lot of problems. He was always invited over to my aunts for Christmas dinner as a gesture.

He and my uncle never saw eye to eye. Well, on this occasion he said something that set off my mom and she simply wanted to leave not having had dinner. My dad refused and she became more and more agitated. It was evident that she was near freaking out on an epic level.

We left after having dinner and my dad was pissed. She seemed and acted like nothing happened and blamed my uncles' brother for saying something "suspicious" and of being in on "it."

No one could escape the witch hunt in her mind. Everyone was against her. Her siblings, her daughters, her husband, strangers that she simply accused of being in on "it." No one was exempt from her baseless accusations.

These episodes would continue for quite some time. There was always something about the Christmas holiday. She would always want to make them hell.

THE COLLEGE YEARS

I would graduate high school and go onto college at the local community college. I hated college to begin with. I couldn't understand why I was paying someone to give me homework and I honestly had no direction at all in my life at that time.

I had no idea what I wanted to be, much less who I was. I had wanted to go directly to the University of Minnesota. I had been accepted, but my mom told me it was a "snob" school and that I was to go to community college.

She told me that I would get "lost" on campus and that I would hate it. Being that I didn't have any experience, much less knowledge about college or what to expect, I believed her. She didn't have any experience either as both my parents were technical school grads.

Consequently, I followed her advice thinking instead I just wasn't good enough or smart enough to make it at the University.

My parents just told my sister and I that we either had to go to college or pay rent. Who the hell wants to pay rent to live at home, so college was the logical choice at the time. With no direction or advice, my sister and I had to navigate the college landscape ourselves.

Luckily, we had to navigate most of our lives ourselves so this was basically nothing new. I took my sister's lead but she would tell me "no one is going to hold your hand." As truth would have it, no one did. I became used to doing things pretty much on my own as I had done most of my life.

I honestly wish I hadn't listened to my mother, but it turned out better as I saved money and didn't end up wasting money on courses I didn't need. I would do that later in life on my journey to find meaning and purpose in my life.

Community college was okay. I had met some friends. I would take a "college" job working for the Dean's secretary. Gosh! No matter what I did for that woman, it was wrong. She absolutely hated me. She couldn't explain things so I could understand them. This was just a relational thing. I would be humiliated on so many levels in that job.

I'd be too scared to ask questions as she would make me feel so stupid. I must have looked like I couldn't do anything correctly. Consequently, I wouldn't be hired for the following year. I was okay with that as I had gotten a job in the Career Center with a boss who was outstanding and like a mother to me.

I would meet so many great people in the Career Center. She would teach me everything about my job but also about life lessons in general.

I would become friends with the person who ran the Phi Theta Kappa group shortly before I graduated from community college. We would do lots of things together but they were the things only she wanted to do. I would want to do things and she wouldn't want to do them ever. I would do things like stay at her house and watch her dogs when she was gone. I hated it as I really only like sleeping in my own bed. I just never knew how to say "no" to her. I went along with it for so long.

One day she called and wanted to go salsa dancing. We had just put a dog down that we had for 16 years. The dog was my childhood pet. It was so hard. I told her that I was too depressed to go and she acted like it was nothing. Things were all about her. I'd had enough and told her I wasn't going. She acted like I was being really, really selfish. Thankfully, she never called again.

This scene would play out over and over again in my life. I always wanted that one person, that one friend who stayed with you for life. I was never able to find that person. I also realized that rarely happens in life. Again, the blessing or a lesson thing.

UNIVERSITY LIFE

I would transfer from the community college to the University of Minnesota in 2000. My mom was totally wrong, I absolutely loved it. I loved the anonymity and the fact that no one knew me. I finally felt like I could do something, that I was proud to be a Gopher and school actually mattered to me.

One day while walking to class, I noticed a booklet on study abroad. Something in me just knew I had to go somewhere. I found a program centered in London. I was hooked the moment I read about it.

My two advisors were totally against it because it would put me behind and I wouldn't graduate on time. That really didn't matter to me because I was set on going.

When I told my mother that I was going to study abroad, she asked me who was going to cook and wash my clothes. She was still doing those things but it wasn't like I couldn't do them myself. It was as if she thought I couldn't do anything in life. That I was "dependent" on her which wasn't even close to true.

I told her that I would be doing those things and she still didn't believe in me. It wasn't like she ever did. Neither of my parents were keen on the idea of me leaving for three months. However, I counted down the days until I was "free" and away from them.

I would leave for London a week before the attacks on the World Trade Center, and the Pentagon. When I left, my parents saw me off from the gate. The country I left that day I never came home to again. I would never see or come home to the country I left on that day again.

I arrived in London and it was quite a shock as I had never been away from home, much less out of the country ever in my life. We arrived at the complex where we would live for three months.

I was assigned to the flat or apartment on the top floor with six other young women. I would pick my room and feel totally and completely alone with strangers from all over the US.

Thankfully, I met one roommate who would become one of my closest friends. She was staying at a hotel with her mom but she was my saving grace. We would become instant friends. I couldn't really relate to the rest of my roommates as they were sorority girls and were simply not on the same page.

We were on a Walk of London that fateful day on September 11, 2001. It had finished so I was getting my books for my courses from a bookstore. When I was walking back to my flat, one of my roommates was listening to a construction worker's radio and she was white as a ghost.

I kept asking her what was wrong, if she was okay. She told me that there had been an attack on the World Trade Center. I had no idea at the time the scale of the attack. I thought it was something like what happened in 1991 or 1992 when a bomb was set off in the parking garage.

The idea that planes were flying into the Trade Center and Pentagon weren't even a thought that crossed my mind.

I would arrive at my flat with everyone watching the news. It seemed like everyone in the program was in our flat. When I arrived I was horrified to watch the second plane fly directly into the second tower along with the collapsing of the two towers. It was heart wrenching to watch knowing I was so far away. There was nothing I could do while people in my country were simply dying.

It seemed so surreal and like something you'd see in a movie. But this was horrifyingly real. I watched people jumping out windows and both the towers collapsed, taking so many innocent lives with them.

One of my roommates said my mom had called and was looking for me. Five minutes after I walked into the door, the phone rang and it was my mom hysterical and wanting me to come home.

I told her that I was basically in the safest place as England had dealt with terrorists from the Irish Republican Army and they were well versed in preventing anything from happening. She finally calmed down enough so I could let her go.

The three months I spent in London were amazing, even with the attack. My roommate and I would explore London, Wales, and Scotland. We were inseparable. The warnings of not to look "American" tainted the trip as England had joined the War on Terror and many people in England did not want to join the war. There were protests everywhere and we were told to avoid them, and to avoid looking like a tourist, especially American tourists.

I also had a law class at Queen Mary University that fall. I would attend a class taught by a magistrate or judge. Our first speaker was about a week after the attacks. We had a woman who was speaking on prostitution and how it should be legalized there.

She totally went off on a tangent against England joining the war. I was the only American in the class. Everyone knew who I was. I could feel 50 eyes on me while she was speaking. I was sinking lower and lower in my chair feeling isolated and blamed.

After class, I was trying to get out without anyone noticing, but there were 5 students from my class who stopped me and told me that they supported me. I was truly amazed and felt like I belonged. I'm truly grateful for those 5 students and I will never forget the comfort they offered me when I felt so targeted.

THE ROAD TO THERAPY

When my trip was coming to a close, I realized that I wouldn't have enough money for my car insurance when I came home. I was on loans and had only enough money to finish the trip. I called my dad and asked if he'd be willing to loan me the money. He told me to get a job so I could pay for it.

This was an impossible task seeing that I was a foreigner and I didn't have a work visa. I tried to explain this but he simply wouldn't hear me. I cried and felt so unworthy and worthless. I couldn't figure out why I wasn't worth it to my dad. Really, I never had been in life, unfortunately. Why he simply wasn't willing to even loan me money. I had never asked for money before or led him to distrust me. He still wouldn't do it no matter how much I begged. Again, Dad only takes. Giving money without the expectation of being paid back is something he never does. Everything given is owed back to him.

One of the program workers found me crying and asked what was wrong. I asked her why I wasn't worth it. She was confused at first and then I told her my dad didn't find me worthy enough to even loan money to. That I didn't have enough money to insure my car and money was really tight until I would arrive home.

She hugged me and tried to comfort me. She told the program director about what had happened. The Director of the program told me that I could work for them and they would pay me under the table.

She also paid for any day trips and events I wanted to go to with no questions asked. She was so amazing and I will always remember what she did for me. I will always be grateful.

I would arrive home right before Christmas that year. I couldn't believe how things had changed. Stores looked like it was the Fourth of July everywhere I went. I didn't recognize the country I arrived back to.

It was so different. People were supportive of each other. People seemed kinder and gentler. Everyone rallied around the flag. It was a symbol of strength and unity at that time. I had never experienced that before.

I would see my psychiatrist for a med review that January. I told him what had happened with my dad and basically that something was very wrong in my life. I couldn't "feel." I knew I was angry and my depression at times would overtake me.

I had been put in therapy in 10th grade. The therapist knew my parents were the problem, but I didn't want to hurt them. I simply said I was all better and stopped the therapy.

I had originally entered therapy in 1998 due to my life being such a mess. A woman who I was working with at the time took me out for dinner. She and I had a heart-to-heart talk. She told me my life could be so much better but that I had to get over the anger, hurt and resentment I had toward my parents. I had to take control of my life. She recommended talk therapy. I will always be grateful to my co-worker as she was the first one to set my on my path of healing and a better life.

I called a mental health clinic that evening. I was able to get in the next week and talk with a woman who would become my first therapist. She recommended meds to which I was against. She also recommended that I meet with a psychiatrist who would end up fitting me well. I would meet the doctor who would be a defining presence for life. He would become like a doctor/dad to me. He still to this day is.

We had gone to Oregon to visit my sister as she had moved out there after getting married. Her husband had gotten a job with Intel there. I told my mom that I was in therapy and that basically she was the reason. She was angry but didn't ruin the trip, amazingly.

I had taken the MMPI (Minnesota Multiphasic Personality Inventory) before I left. Some of the questions I had to think about so long were questions like "My mother is a good person." "My father is a good person" etc.

When I arrived back from Oregon, I had an appointment with my therapist again and I told her that something was really, really wrong in my life. I made fists and was just so angry when I talked about my family.

I hated and loathed myself and life in general. She told me that I was living in a prison of my own making. That I had the key to leave but I was simply so stuck that I couldn't find the door or the key that were both in plain sight.

I don't remember why I stopped seeing her but I was simply going for medication evaluations with my psychiatrist and this was simply not enough. I needed intensive talk therapy for the rage, shame, endless amounts of emotional pain, anger and depression I was experiencing on a daily basis.

When I arrived back from London, my original therapist had left the practice so my psychiatrist asked if I would be willing to work with him. I agreed and this would be the beginning of a 23-year doctor/patient relationship. It would end up changing my life for the better and forever.

He would see me through some of the most traumatic events in my life. We would go through the trauma, anger and pain I experienced up to that point taking it apart layer by layer. I would see him every two weeks for about 21 years. I owe him so much. Actually, I owe him my life. He has been a saving grace to me on so many levels.

My doctor would become a defining presence in my life. He would take a very broken twentysomething and would eventually transform her into a very functional individual.

I had been broken for so long. The pain and agony had layers upon layers of resentment, anger, shame, and humiliation to sort through. Family dynamics would be explored along with the way I thought about things in general.

I would learn that things were not my fault. I would slowly take the perfect persona I had created back in school and bring out the woman I had shoved down and been ashamed to be for so long. I would heal her and find her worthy of being. However, it would be a very long road to recovery.

GRADUATION AND MOM STRIKES AGAIN

I graduated from college in the fall of 2002. Mom was again paranoid and accusing people of being in on "it." Again, we had no idea what that "it" was. "It" was getting really, really old whatever "it" was. She would hide in the interior hallway of the house thinking that people were shooting at her.

She would hold the dog hostage in the hallway with her. The poor dog wet the carpet because mom wouldn't let him go outside. This episode would last into the winter of that year.

She would also tell some crazy story of how her late father was in the mafia and that somehow the mafia was after her. My grandfather died when my mother was four. He was a drug salesman for Pfizer.

His death back then created a huge void in the family as to be expected. My grandmother, for some reason, couldn't get over his death and was committed to a mental hospital for months at a time. Needless to say, my mothers' claims were beyond bizarre and only made sense to her.

I again had mom brought to the hospital by ambulance and put on police lock-up. They kept her for a few days. I never knew what was so wrong but I would graduate college while she was committed.

On the Saturday of commencement, she kept calling every five minutes to find out how the dog was. I was so angry and irritated that I called her hospital floor asking for them to take the phone away from her. This only pissed her off more but I was so angry and resentful that I really didn't care.

For some reason, it didn't occur to me to take the phone off the hook. I was so upset and hurt. I would have my dad, 2 friends and a mentor attend the ceremony but the hurt inflicted from mom would cast a shadow over the event. It was yet another of many, many "shitty mom things."

When I was to walk across the stage, I was crying. I just wanted to get across without anyone noticing. Unfortunately, the Regent who shook my hand saw and asked me to smile as this was "my day."

He would have no clue how much pain I was in or how angry I was that one of the most important events in my life yet again didn't include and was again all about my mom and her issues. Again, she played center stage.

I would explode at my dad as he had given me a graduation card with money with both of their names signed on it. I couldn't figure out how he could even still love her at this point. He basically ignored me and told me to settle down. That it wasn't a big deal. The thing is, it was.

My mother had put herself center stage for so long It just became sickening and so tiring. She had ruined so many milestones, holidays and other events up to this point that I had enough.

I just couldn't fathom and I still can't understand how he could even defend her even now. It was incomprehensible that he would defend her after all she has done to him, my sister and me through the years.

I don't know why I let my mothers situation ruin my milestone day as she wouldn't care anyway. I guess when you finish college you expect your parents to be proud of you. Not so, in my case.

My mom cared more about her dog than she did about me or my achievement. This would continue to be an ongoing thing in my life. The dog would take precedence over me and still does even to this day.

Mom would come out of the hospital like nothing happened and we would live life like we usually did avoiding the elephant in the room. We never talked about family issues as everything was always swept under the rug even when the rug was atop a mound so high it hit the ceiling.

Mom simply couldn't handle hearing about how her behavior affected us and she just didn't care.

The only one my mother ever cared about was herself. She cannot handle being told that something is offensive or handling boundaries. She has no boundaries to this day. My Dad will never stick up to her or support me in going up against her.

He will sit and watch and listen to her lies and justification for doing horrible things. He has never stood up for me. He has sat there and watched her try to rip me to shreads. He'll apologize for her bad behavior but he will never stick up for me. It's just not enough. However, my sister is a different story. She will do anything for her.

She hasn't broke me. She won't ever get the pleasure of doing that. It really pisses her off. Every time I go up against her I win. I will no longer take her disrespect, bullshit claims, backstabbing or lies she likes to tell.

I used to get really hurt by this. I don't blame my sister as it is not her fault. It's his. You don't play favorites with your kids. If my sister were to murder me, he would stand by and defend her. Somehow the murder would be my fault. But I realize that it's him and it is not a reflection of who I am in any way.

In the long run, it has made me extremely emotionally and mentally strong. Dad will receive his Karma sooner rather than later. For now, I'm content with being who I am regardless of his favoritism.

I have learned to never do this to my children when I have them. It is such a devastating blow and really affects self-worth and self-esteem that can take years of therapy to repair. I have learned to separate myself from my parents and that their horrible behavior is a reflection of them, not me.

It has taken me 32 years to overcome the trauma and shame inflicted upon me. I'm really proud of the person I've become and I know it had nothing to do with them.

My mom couldn't figure out why I needed therapy. She had gone several times over the years before, but never stuck with it. Therapy makes you look at yourself and face the pain you have not only been through but also that you have caused.

It makes you deal with the pain endured and is a way of making you change your behavior. In the end, if you stick with it, your life improves and you become a better person.

That is not something my mother is willing to do. Only taking the anti-depressants will not change behavior or cure pain. It is only a temporary fix. I fully believe you need talk therapy to really change or heal. She's not one to believe that she caused any pain or needs to change. She believes everyone else causes her actions; it's always everyone else's fault and never hers.

When my mother was abusing prescription drugs we would tell the doctor who was prescribing them to stop giving them to her. It fell on deaf ears. I hated her doctor. I still do. The "Quack" just kept pumping my mother full of drugs that she used to get "high." She was terrible and believed whatever my mom told her.

We were desperate to get her into a program or rehab but her doctor just wouldn't listen. Mom showed up to work high and lost her nursing license. She also hit a doctor's BMW which was a hit on the car insurance.

4 weeks after my dad bought a new 2009 malibu she ran a stop sign and smashed in the front end. She wanted to get it to the shop before my dad came home so we drove to Abra Autobody. As she was driving the car, parts of it were flying off of it.

Had the police been called by the other driver, she would have been charged with DUI and probably forced to enter a rehab program. The other driver didn't but he also didn't submit a claim against my dad's insurance.

You can't force someone into rehab. It has to be their choice unless a court assigns it. We didn't talk about

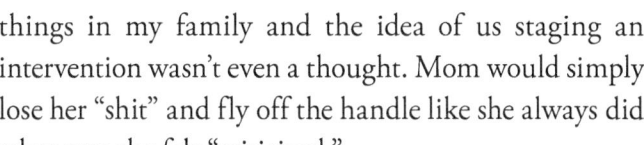

things in my family and the idea of us staging an intervention wasn't even a thought. Mom would simply lose her "shit" and fly off the handle like she always did whenever she felt "criticized."

She would fall off the deep end and the "wrath" would be horrible. Not to mention she didn't see a problem and she does whatever she wants no matter who it harms.

FAMILY HISTORY AND TRAUMA

My mother grew up with a single mother. Her father passed away when she was 4 years old. She had three other siblings; a sister and two brothers. Her mother was obviously devastated but more so than she probably should have been. The woman just could not cope with life after grandpa died.

My grandmother lived to die. After Grandpa died, she ended up in a mental institution for 6 months. My mom's older two siblings had to take care of things. My aunt still resents that she had to grow up before her time. It's been over 50 years and she's still angry as hell. Mom was the youngest so her siblings took care of her.

My grandmother didn't get better until my mom was 13 and even then she would tell my mom that my mom could come to the cemetery with a rocking chair and talk to her. That's not really something you tell your 13 year old.

Grandma died before my sister and I were born. Our older cousins knew her but I get the feeling that she was very dependent on my Grandfather. When he passed away she simply stopped living. She lived to die. I have a strong suspicion that she died of a broken heart.

She never dated after he died, they never went on trips as a family after grandpa died. They were simply a broken family. Without grandpa, grandma stopped living and the whole family dynamic fell apart.

My mom found grandma dead on the bathroom floor when she was 18. I cannot imagine how horrible that would be. My mom would not only lose her mother but also her place to live and her stability. Her siblings simply wanted to sell everything to get the money. Mom was an afterthought, sadly. The two older siblings; my uncle and my aunt were the greediest. My aunt thought she was entitled to more than she actually was.

Mom would have to move in with her sister and her family. My aunt is not the nicest person. They fought a lot, so my mom wanted to get out. My parents decided to get married. Not the best decision.

All the children in that family married young and the two boys married toxic women. Both would end up getting divorced. The oldest brother was simply toxic and was a bully in the family. He's still toxic and has made some really shitty decisions in life. He is a sarcastic, egotistical asshole who I want nothing to do with.

About a year before my grandmother died, my mom was in a horrible car accident where she was hit by a drunk driver. The laws back then were not as harsh as they are now. Mom was thrown from the car and was put in traction for 6 months. I often wonder if some of her impulsivity and bad decision-making is due to the head trauma she received from the accident. It would explain a lot but not excuse the trauma she has caused.

As for my dad, grandpa was an ass. I get the feeling that his upbringing wasn't roses. Grandpa favored my aunt. I get the feeling that Grandpa forced my dad to fix broken things and simply did not give anything to his son emotionally or monetarily. My dad is really good with mechanical things like cars among other things.

Unfortunately, I did not inherit those skills. Grandpa wouldn't play with my aunt and dad when they were little as he was more interested in going to the bar with his buddies and leaving my grandma to take care of his kids.

My grandpa basically forced my dad into the railroad because of the pension through the government. Wow! That pension was well worth the deadly accidents, horrible management and abusive bosses that would turn my dad into such a cold, unfeeling person.

I honestly hate the railroad for the inhumane way they treat their workers. There is a huge problem in

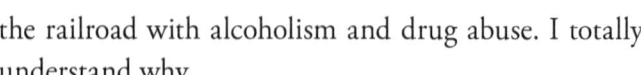

the railroad with alcoholism and drug abuse. I totally understand why.

Unfortunately, my dad took my grandfather's advice and would work for the heartless people at the railroad. Nevermind that he could have made more money in construction than he would ever make at the railroad. Grandpa knew best…right?

I would watch my dad try to get Grandpa's acceptance and love. It truly broke my heart as I was trying to do the same thing with him. My sister was always the star of the show so I totally knew how he felt. Dad never received it, unfortunately. Grandpa sucked as both a dad and a grandfather. The man was cold and unfeeling. However, if you were my sister, or my younger cousin, you were loved. Fuck that shit!

Needless to say, I never followed my grandfather's advice. He always said my sister could be a financial analyst and I could be someone's secretary. Again, grandpa was never someone I wanted to get close with. He favored my sister and my one cousin. I was never "good enough" in his eyes.

JOBS AT THE UNIVERSITY

I had been working for the University of Minnesota as I had been hired in the winter of 2002 in the Engineering school. I had a very overdramatic boss who was trying to be an actress. She came into this dream later in life. She was truly into drama personally and professionally.

Mind you she was in her 60's. She went as far as to get a face lift so she could be in commercials or film or whatever she wanted. She was in some plays and one Ragu commercial I never saw, but she thought she was the shit.

She didn't really like me and the office dynamic was very toxic. In truth, I think she was jealous of me because I received my degree and she didn't have one. She was just a really, really unhappy and toxic person. She was on the road to retirement and simply didn't want to do her job. She would take personal calls from her sister all the time. Drama was basically her middle name.

She was an advisor and they were going to make it mandatory that the person who took over her job when she retired would have to have a masters degree. I think she was insulted by that but I agreed. Advisors should have at least a masters degree to advise students who are getting bachelors degrees.

She would constantly complain about how this guy she was on again and off again wouldn't commit. She would talk to others in the office (except me as I tried to avoid her drama). I think she spent more time trying to determine what she should do with this guy rather than doing her job which was to advise students. I would leave that job for a better opportunity in a different Engineering department. Before I left, I was invited to her retirement party where she wanted people to donate money for an expensive diamond bracelet or something along those lines as her gift.

I thought it was obnoxious and selfish of her to insist that people pay for that. I didn't bother going as I just had too much of her in the two years I worked there. She was so very full of herself.

I would start my new department in 2004 working as an Executive Assistant. I would gain a large head and cause drama myself. I'm not proud of the person I became and I'm truly sorry for any pain I caused. Truth be told, I was still trying to overcome my trauma, though that is not an excuse.

My boss there was better and didn't cause too much drama but she played favorites. I loved that job for a while until my boss recommended I try to find something that I would enjoy better and that was less stressful. She told me that I seemed unhappy and maybe a job change would be beneficial for me. I really wish I hadn't taken her advice.

I looked on the university's job board and applied for one in Housing and Residential Life I thought might be fun. I interviewed and ended up getting the position to my detriment. I was trained by several individuals and systems never seemed to work correctly.

Some were archaic like the payroll system and I never really learned how to navigate it. I would get calls weekly from the woman in the payroll department telling me that I had done it wrong or that someone was missing a punch. She was the worst person to train me. I was so lost when she showed me the system that I had no clue what I was doing.

I would be isolated in this position in an office with no other people. I hated it. I hated my boss even more. He was nice to begin with but then just became more and more abusive to me. I hated the events of the year with a passion.

I started the job in February. I really enjoyed working with the students but hated hiring students and having to find someone to cover the student front desk all the time. I hated doing the schedules, payroll and tracking down rented equipment.

The maintenance crew hated me. Especially the guy that was assigned to the building and his gang of simpletons. They were just cruel. The head of maintenance informed me that I was responsible for changing over the keys or putting them in a different order at the end of the school year.

He explained it so poorly that I asked my summer student to do it to see if he could understand. During the summer the dorms turn into housing for different teams and people that are looking for somewhere cheap to stay. I had to get key cards, mailbox keys and bathroom signs changed over. None of this I had been trained correctly on so nothing was done correctly.

My boss was becoming more and more abusive by the day. I started to loath Mondays and celebrate Fridays. Evidently, my summer student didn't understand how to do the keys correctly either as all the keys were wrong when the fall semester started. I was blamed for it. It was just another nail in my coffin and another step on the way to "failing" employee probation.

My boss's abuse would be more than I could handle. The fact that I had no friends and I was isolated was even worse. I had no one to talk to and I was becoming more and more depressed and despondent as time went on. I started missing more and more work. I just couldn't go there and take the emotional and mental abuse.

One day I asked how I was doing in my job and my boss said we would have "feedback meetings" to go over things. I learned that these were simply meetings to tear me down. He would simply tell me all the things that I was doing wrong and rip me to shreds. I obviously learned to hate and fear these meetings. He would then send me an email documententing everything we discussed. It was so humiliating.

I was calling in more and more and calling my doctor to help me cope on a daily basis until that fateful day in September when I couldn't promise his nurse that I wouldn't hurt myself. Yet again I couldn't force myself to go to work. It was too painful and humiliating. The shame at my perceived weaknesses was paralyzing.

I had been looking for another position but I came off as desperate in the interviews and that is not attractive to potential employers. I would end up in the hospital on suicide watch cold and alone in the emergency room for 8 hours that fateful day.

Karma would come to my boss as he moved down to Florida to become head of housing Judicial Affairs at a University. He really liked to punish people so this was his dream job. Anyway, he had found a guy that he really liked and wanted to marry.

They had bought rings at Tiffanies of all places. One day my boss's boyfriend said he was going to go and stay at their cabin in the woods. My boss, wanting to "surprise" his lover, drove up to the cabin and found his partner in bed with another man. Needless to say, they did not end up getting married.

My boss also was in a relationship with someone when I worked in the department. His partner was so kind. On occasion I had to go on outings with the Resident Assistants. For one outing, I had to go ice skating. I had never ice skated. I was terrified of falling or breaking a leg.

My boss's partner took my hand and taught me how to ice skate. He was such a kind guy. I couldn't figure out what he was doing with my boss. I found out later that he ghosted my boss. He was worth so much more than what my boss could offer anyway. I wish him well and hope that he found a partner worthy of him as my boss wasn't even close.

THE HOSPITAL AND THE BEGINNING OF A LONG RECOVERY

I was eventually brought up to the mental health ward and I wasn't as bad off as some of the other patients but that didn't mean I didn't have issues that I needed to deal with. I would be roommates with a woman from California who had plans to row out in the ocean and kill herself with a gun, but thankfully ended up on the ward instead.

Her employer would not stop calling her while she was there. I can certainly see why she hated her employer. I hated mine too. I would end up on FMLA until the end of October that year.

My youngest nephew was born while I was in the hospital. I still can't remember if his birthday is September 26 or 27 due to the trauma. My sister had called that morning and said that she had a baby boy and that they named him Daniel.

She said he's not a "Dan" or a "Danny" that he would be called Daniel. She told me that I had to get better because she wanted me to see her son and watch him grow up. I still get tears in my eyes when I recall the memory of that call. It was so very painful.

The decision to move forward and face life was mine and it was so painful. Death seemed like an easier answer, but thankfully I didn't take that route. I'm truly grateful as I would have missed some of the most important, beautiful and most meaningful moments in my life up to this point.

The emotion was so raw and I was in so much pain and mental turmoil. She told me that I had nephews that I had to see grow up. However, the pain was incredibly intense and survival seemed impossible. I had hit rock bottom. I would either get better or die. I really wasn't sure how to get better but death was no longer a choice I wanted to make.

One of the nights in the hospital, I was crying and one of the nurses came and talked to me. She said that I would have to start my life over. That I would need to leave my job. I hated my boss and my job, but I couldn't simply leave.

She told me that I should work in something like a flower shop or something along those lines with less stress and more mental peace. All I could think of was that I had rent among other bills that I needed to pay. How could I work for less than I was making? I was already stretched so thin moneywise. I couldn't just leave my job.

I would come off FMLA but tried to avoid going back to work at all costs. I was in and out of the hospital but they finally told me that I couldn't hide there. I would have to face my problems and climb centimeter by centimeter up from the bottom of the hell I was in. This would be no easy task. Satan was a mighty strong and daming dance partner. I would come out stronger, with burn scars, a map and the ability to endure the heat hell offered.

I would return to work the week before the Thanksgiving holiday. My horrible boss didn't say anything or seem happy that I was back. The abuse would continue and I would miss part of that week and the next.

When I came in the Wednesday before Thanksgiving he came into my office and closed the door. He handed me a letter saying that I had failed employee probation and that I was no longer employed. Employee probation lasts a year at the University and I started Housing in February. I would be placed on the layoff list but basically, I didn't have a job anymore.

The shame and humiliation were overwhelming. I had been packing up my stuff for a while hoping that I would bring it back to a new position but that didn't happen. I walked to the bathroom, looked in the mirror and felt relieved. I packed up what was left of my desk and walked to my car and drove home. The abuse ended but the road forward would be filled with fear, pain, shame, triumph and freedom.

We had family over for Thanksgiving that year. My cousin's wife had just gotten a new job and she was starting that Monday. I remember thinking that I didn't have anywhere to be expected because I no longer had a job to go to. I felt directionless and feared for my future. I had a lease and I hated being alone in my apartment. I felt completely and utterly alone.

I know what it is like to be lonely. I've been in the company of many people and also still felt totally and completely alone. I felt that way many times during my recovery. I would move back home with my parents to offset the loneliness I often felt. This wouldn't be my only experience with loneliness during my long recovery. It would stalk me throughout and during the most challenging times of my life.

DIALECTICAL BEHAVIOR THERAPY

Before I had the experience in the hospital, I was attending Dialectical Behavior Group Therapy. My doctor recommended it. Those women in that group were and would be my support network. DBT as it is known is a therapy for people who suffer from Borderline Personality Disorder. It is a therapy used to help regulate emotions.

I would go every week and use the same healing technique "Self-Soothe" and "Radical Acceptance" Both are tools to deal with the curve balls life throws at you. They are both emotional regulation tools to help cope with difficult life events rather than exploding or making things worse.

You basically let harmful thoughts and feelings pass like waves in the ocean. You make a kit for these times of scents, oils etc or simply do something you enjoy doing like taking a hot bath or shower, reading a book or calling a friend to make yourself feel better.

At that time those women were all I had. Every week, I had interviews and every week I had been turned down. I was never judged, they were always supportive.

I learned how to regulate my emotions but I also learned how supportive group therapy is. I needed those women at that time. I stuck with the therapy which was one or two years. You go through each section of the therapy twice.

The women in that group were some of the bravest women I had ever met. Some had been through much worse trauma than that which I had been through. I would lean on these women and they would lean on me for support. It was an environment that I needed at that time in my life. They would help me change for the better.

Even after being turned down for position after position, they were always there for me. Even encouraging me to keep going. I will always be grateful for the women in my group and the two facilitators. I know not all of the women were able to make it through the full therapy as it is rather intense.

But, I made it all the way through and learned the techniques. It was a life changing experience. God always puts people in your path who you need and I needed the support of these amazing women at that time. I felt so alone and needed to feel supported. They gave me that support I needed for which I am forever grateful.

WORKING MY WAY UP FROM THE BOTTOM

I would find a job working for Target at minimum wage, making half of what I made at the University. Amazingly, I stayed there for about 2 years. Working retail came easy for me as I'm really a people person.

I liked meeting new people and enjoyed working with so many great people. This was during the recession.

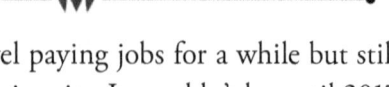

I would hold low-level paying jobs for a while but still be applying to the University. It wouldn't be until 2017 that I would finally land a full-time position.

In 2007, I returned to the University of Minnesota to finish my masters degree that I had started back in 2004. My degree was in Human Resource Development. I was beside myself to get out of the low paying jobs I had been in. I needed to make more money to survive and I was just really lost. Going back and finishing my degree, I thought, was the answer.

However, the economy would have a different idea. The "crash" or "near crash" of the US economy would work against me. I worked hard to finish my degree. I wasn't really interested in it but I thought with a masters degree I "surely" would find a better job. I was so wrong. Competition was so fierce for jobs at that time, no matter what I did, I couldn't get hired.

I'm horrible at interviewing and I really hate bragging about myself. I am an introvert and I find it really hard to talk myself up as it just seems so rude. This is the whole point of an interview so you can tell them all the great things you did and how great you are.

I hate interviewing with a passion. Consequently, I wouldn't get hired because of this. Interview after interview I would be rejected or turned down.

I hate attention being on me or being the center of attention. I hate really loud places and I will never be the life of a party. I think really loud, boisterous people are obnoxious and I choose to avoid being around them.

I prefer a quiet night at home rather than a party, bar or any other social gathering. I like small, intimate gatherings. I hate big gatherings like weddings, big birthday parties, or any other gathering where there are more than 3-4 people.

This was such a frustrating time in my life. I felt lost and unemployable. I would leave Target to go to a before- and after-school daycare in my local school district. I would work there for 3 years and have yet another horrible experience with one of my bosses. I would work 2 hours a day and earn really low pay, thus barely getting by.

I learned I hated working in a daycare. Kids don't listen because their parents don't enforce rules at home. Kids are just mean to each other and I would get so burned out at this job.

During the summer of 2009, we would have the kids all day. At the school I was at, we would make mistake after mistake after mistake. One day we had a slip-n-slide outside, and we forgot to have the kids put on sunscreen or something happened where not all of them had it on that day.

One little boy received a 2-3 degree sunburn and his family would sue the daycare. We all had to make statements to lawyers or some other people who came and were part of the court. I felt horrible. That summer was hell for me. One thing after another just went wrong.

In the fall of 2011, I would work at a different school. I would have a supervisor who was full of himself and just hated me. I didn't have much experience with kids so I observed others who worked there. The school that I was at was so much different than the one I had been at during the previous year. It was well run but it was like a gestapo.

My boss wanted to be a teacher but I can see why he was never hired. He constantly criticized me and he seemed too much like my former boss in housing. Nothing I ever did was good enough or it was totally wrong etc. This situation seemed so familiar to me that I knew I couldn't stay there.

He would eventually set up a meeting with me and HR to go over how to "better my performance." My boss at my previous school queued me into the fact that he wanted me fired. If I stayed at the school I was at, he would find a way to fire me.

I would leave the school I was at and go back to my previous school. I would work 2 hours a day which was barely enough to pay my bills. I again would feel trapped. The hamster wheel I was on just kept going and I was truly going nowhere.

That winter of 2011 mom would start her prescription drug addiction. Truly, it started earlier like in 2005 but we just simply couldn't get her to go to treatment.

I was on Xanax for anxiety at that time. Unbeknownst to me, she was taking my pills. I would run out before the fill date which I found really strange because I wasn't using them every day.

My dad started hiding the pills in my room in odd places so she wouldn't find them. I would come home to a room that had been ripped apart and things just simply not where I had put them.

My dad finally put the pills in my purse to throw her off track. One morning I was leaving for work and I put the pills on the end table in the living room. I mistakenly left them there. When I came home from work, I found my mother on her hands and knees holding a broken handle to a coffee cup and totally babbling nonsense. She was so out of it that I had to remove her from the top of the stairs fearing she would go head-first down them.

I'd finally had enough! I called 911 and told them that she had overdosed. They came and she was so out of it that she couldn't figure out why the police and ambulance were there much less why I was so angry.

I called my dad at work and told him basically to get his ass home. I was so tired of this scene and it had played out so many times. I was simply exhausted and couldn't do it anymore.

Needless to say, he did not come home. I did not go to see my mother in the hospital and I still won't as she was not there for me when I desperately needed someone when I was so low and life was so challenging.

Mom has had various joint replacements; shoulder replacement, hip replacements-twice and knee replacements. She's basically made of all metal now. She complains continuously about pain.

She is obese and doctors have told her to lose some weight which really pisses her off. She thinks all the weight is because she stopped smoking 10-12 years ago. That was 10 TO 12 YEARS AGO! What basis that has now, I have no clue.

She tells her doctors that she will simply start smoking again if they continue to insist that she lose weight. What a great solution! Ruin your health further to solve a simple problem of just needing diet and exercise.

My mom is just plain LAZY! She didn't want to work so she claimed railroad disability 15 years before she could have and should have retired. This was probably one of the worst decisions she could have ever made.

She just simply didn't want to work anymore. She complained relentlessly about her pain and suffering to doctors to get a double hip replacement. The disability claim was granted, unfortunately.

Mom would rather take a pill than fix the overall problem. Unfortunately, a lot of Americans think the way she does. It's why we have such a dependence on prescription drugs and why the drug companies make so much money.

Why put in the work if a pill can fix everything. If that were true, all of us would be fit, healthy and happy. Nothing could be farther from the truth. Fact is, if you take a pill there are always side effects. When you change or try to fix one thing in the body something else is always affected. You fix one problem but potentially cause another.

Give me a pill to solve every little issue I have. My back hurts, give me an Oxy. I can't concentrate, give me Adderall. I have a headache! Give me migraine medication. I'm not trying to undermine people, but if Americans would eat healthier and exercise, we'd be healthier and happier as a nation.

We are so much larger body-wise than any other nation in the world. Our diets are killing us. The obesity rate in the US is just so embarrassing and the amount of people with type 2 diabetes, heart failure, all types of cancer, strokes and heart attacks is beyond belief. I don't believe any other nation has the amount of diet-related health issues we have in the U.S.

Give me the drug that will fix it! Nevermind that I have a gut that hangs over my waist. Nevermind that I'm severely obese. Give me the pill! Exercise? Who the hell wants to do that?

My mom has always been that way. She taught me that a pill can fix everything. It's simply not true. We need to put in the work to change. There are no shortcuts, no free rides. It's putting in the work plain and simple. This is something she just refuses to do along with many, many other people in our population.

ENCOUNTERS OF A HORRIBLE KIND

For the final project for my HRD degree, I had to do an internship. To try and find a company that I could intern with and possibly be hired after I graduated, I had attended the yearly University Job Fair.

There I would get contact information for an insurance person from an Insurance company. He was really interested in recruiting agents for his "business" and would hire me to help him recruit. Being that I was still quite lost in life and was still really messed up, I would develop a crush on him. This would be a very regrettable experience for me.

I would work for him that summer and work my butt off for $8 an hour. I felt so slimy in that job. It wasn't really a job we were recruiting people for, it was to be an insurance agent for the company and it really was more like a scam.

I would try to recruit people any way I could. We were going on job sites like Careerbuilder and Monster.

We were calling people making it look like this great opportunity. I worked my ass off because I knew if I could bring people through the door he would hire me. I desperately needed a job as I was graduating that fall.

I'm ashamed that I looked through resumes of people who were nurses, lawyers, accountants among other professions simply looking for another job because they had lost their livelihood in the recession.

I felt so dirty but I did it knowing that I didn't have any other options. Full-time jobs and hiring were basically at a standstill. People were desperate and I was offering false hope. I still regret doing it. I truly wish I had never worked for or met the agent on so many levels.

People he recruited would have to pay to set up agencies and it just was really kind of shady. No one wanted to do it and he had trouble recruiting people because it wasn't really a paying "job." It was a "business" opportunity that relatively few people succeeded at.

One Saturday, he invited me to come over to his house to watch a football game and I took it like he "liked" me. One day I went back to his house again, unannounced. I stayed for a while and he asked if I wanted to go upstairs and watch TV in his room so he could fall asleep.

Me, being totally clueless (I had never been asked that question before or thought that it was an invitation for sex. I was quite naive back then. I've since learned.). We ended up having sex (which I regret). In my mind, I thought that meant that he "loved" me. For me, at that time, sex and love went together. I was so wrong and completely ashamed.

I couldn't comprehend that he had used me. In a phone call, he apologized as I was still a virgin at that time. I was hysterical. I couldn't believe that I had given something sacred to me for his cheap thrill.

I was devastated. I thought that if I could "prove" my love, he would see that he loved me. This would be a huge mistake. I did not know then that you don't chase men. If they truly care and want to be with you, they will come to you. He simply had taken advantage of me and used me for his pleasure.

I was quite messed up as I said. I would make a huge mistake and send him things in the mail hoping he would "fall in love with me." I sincerely regret this. I did finally figure it out that he would never "love" me but I had lost something I had hoped to give to someone I loved and who loved me back. Again, the pairing of sex and love. Now, I realize that they are two different things and are not always paired together. It was a very painful lesson to learn.

I was so ashamed of myself and felt so stupid for a long time. The thing I didn't know is that you have to love and respect yourself first before anyone else can love you. This would be a hard lesson to learn as I loathed myself at that time.

FINDING MY WAY

I spent the next few months/years again trying to find a full-time job. This was during the recession. I was getting so discouraged. There seemed to be hundreds of people applying for the same jobs at that time. I became so frustrated that I decided to go back to school for teaching. I had been accepted at a small, private school.

I would also regret this decision. I would attend for 1.5 years and get tired and disenchanted. The school was just not for me and I felt I wasn't getting my money's worth.

The instructors were all school teachers with master's degrees and something just never felt right. It felt too easy. I was used to the rigor of the University I attended before. I would learn to hate the school and never finish my degree and waste a huge amount of money.

While I was attending school, I was working as a reading tutor for AmeriCorps. I made very little money and worked with children K-5 helping to improve their reading skills. I just hated it.

Everything was the same daily and I hate doing the exact same thing day after day. I would do this for a year and two months and all for very little pay. I would leave that paid volunteer position in October of 2013.

In August of that year, I had a bad argument with my mother and made the bad decision to move out. I would end up moving down to Bloomington, MN and living with a roommate who ended up being an alcoholic. I would work two jobs and still not have enough to live on.

I was exhausted daily and I hated it. One day I would call my car insurance agent letting him know that I would be late on my payment. I just happened to mention that I was looking for a full time job.

He would end up interviewing me and hiring me in November of that year. I thought it was a Godsend at that time. I would end up disliking it and being put under pressure to sell policies I didn't believe in to make money for the agent. I would stay until June of that year. I was often stressed out. I couldn't take time off because he viewed time off as something people do if they aren't loyal.

He didn't pay vacation until someone had been there a year and it was only one week. He was so dedicated to his business that he expected extreme loyalty from his employees, too. I get loyalty, but not at the expense of personal wellbeing. I would leave the agency for a teaching job at an inner city school which I would hate even more.

I started working at a charter school in July of that year. I spent the month in orientation and thought it was for me until the students came back. The school year started in August because many of the children didn't have anywhere to go over the summer as their parents usually couldn't afford daycare.

I would have many issues with this school as I wasn't a full fledged teacher and I was expected to stay over hours to get the classroom ready among other things without overtime pay. The school day was 8 hours and I had kids falling asleep during class because they didn't get enough sleep at home.

The kids came from troubled families and had behavioral issues that I simply hated dealing with and I was paired with a teacher who had no experience in the classroom except from student teaching. It was an absolute nightmare to say the least.

The director of the school had this goal of beating the test scores of the number one school located in Wayzata, Minnesota. Today, the schools in Wayzata are still number 1 in overall test scores. It's where all the wealthy kids attend. The school I worked for is still at the bottom or close to the bottom even to this day.

I became quite sick one day and told the secretary that I was leaving. She said okay, so I left. I went to school the next week and was called into HR. I knew what was coming, as this job simply was not for me. I hated the school, the kids and didn't believe in the mission of the school to begin with. I was let go. Surprisingly, I really just didn't care. The job wasn't meant for me.

It was a relief as I didn't want to be there to begin with, thus I never finished my teaching degree. At least one teacher that I had started with and one other that had been there awhile all quit in September. It was truly a toxic place to work and they had very high teacher turnover, unsurprisingly.

During this time, loneliness and depression were a huge problem as I felt like a failure because I simply couldn't find a job that was fit for me. I would move back in with my parents and stay for a while. Mom and I would fight and I would learn to not react to her outbursts of anger and rage. I still desperately wanted to get out and eventually I would.

For my next job, I would end up interviewing at Wells Fargo for a phone banker position. I would get it, and hate that also. I stayed 6 months. In those six months I would have horrible anxiety, be humiliated for not selling on quota and absolutely hate my job.

Wells would be charged with opening accounts for customers without their permission among other horrible acts because they used threats and humiliation to push their employees to meet sales quotas.

I left a week before the scandal broke. It didn't surprise me as I had been humiliated for the same reason while I was there. It was an absolutely horrible nightmare to work there.

They have since been accused of doing other things against banking policy all in the name of keeping the customer and making it more difficult for them to go to another bank. Because of their lacking morals, more customers have probably left and they have been charged millions upon millions of dollars to make up for lying and cheating, but more than likely haven't admitted any wrongdoing or held anyone accountable for their bullying and wrongdoing.

I woke up one morning in August and just knew I couldn't work there anymore. My overall health was deteriorating and my anxiety was so bad that I had to go back on anti-anxiety medication. I had been off of it for many years.

My parents kept telling me to stay there. That I could climb the ladder into something better but things just kept getting worse. That day I drove to the office and sat in my car. I just couldn't bring myself to do it another day.

I went into the front door where security was located and gave them my badge and told them it was my last day. They took it and I walked out. I had no idea where I was going or how I was going to make a living. All that I knew was that I couldn't work for Wells anymore. So I left.

I drove to my family church and sat in the parking lot and cried and prayed. I prayed to God saying that if he could lead me, I would follow his way. I then went home and sat on the front step trying to figure out what I was going to tell my parents. They knew I hated it, but I knew that they also believed one should never quit a job before having another one.

I told my mom and she didn't say anything. I told my dad and he was disappointed in me. I have learned that a job, is a job, is a job. Life is too short to hate your job. It's 40 hours every week. That is too much time to be doing something you hate. I'm not sacrificing my mental health and wellbeing for a job ever again. It's just not worth it.

After my stint at Wells, I went to work at Walmart as a shoes and jewelry associate. I hated that too, but it was a job. I liked the people who worked there but I hated the job. I made $13 an hour, enough to pay the bills but I was tired of retail, and simply didn't want to do it anymore. I felt so trapped. I would again apply at the University.

Amazingly, I received a call for an interview in March of 2017. I went and it was so easy for me. I ended up getting the job but unbeknownst to me my boss would be an ongoing issue. I would work with her and a colleague who was my boss's best buddy. It would be a horrible experience. I would start looking for positions one year after getting the position. Again, I would look desperate and no one would hire me. The whole bragging thing in the interview just didn't suit me.

My colleague would get married the year I started and eventually become pregnant. She would go on maternity leave and quit in August of 2019. They hired a former student who previously held my position for my colleague's old position. I had applied but I gave up when I found out they had someone in mind who wasn't me.

Instead, I would go for a reclassification to move into a higher position. My boss would be of little help in the process. She would rate me so low that I didn't have enough points to make it to be reclassed. However, our HR person intervened and had me change the points in certain areas so that I would be approved.

The person who would next become my colleague would be a Godsend. She is and was amazing. My boss favored her over me also. However, she disliked my boss too, so she would tell me the things my boss was doing and saying behind my back.

COVID hit, we worked from home, and my boss was really old school and liked to micromanage us. It was suffocating. She would degrade me and my position during this time. My colleague and I would have to put up with endless phone calls from our supervisor making sure we were doing our jobs. She also liked to gossip about others in the office.

She would make comments about my weight as I was slimming down but they were more like disguised insults. She would say how her daughter was gaining weight. Her daughter was trying to have a baby and was on medication to help conceive.

My boss would say the cruelest things not only to me but also about her daughter. My weight gain was due to my binge eating disorder. It was something I struggled with since childhood but she was again, too ignorant to think about that. I do not like or trust my now former supervisor. She was just mean and mean for no reason. She abused power and was basically toxic.

My colleague forwarded an email from my boss saying that she was going to give me the "grunt" work that was required for our accreditation, which she did. My new colleague would leave just over a year later.

I would take over her position and eventually be hired in it. My boss would dump work on me, pretending to be "my friend." I saw right through it and would be fake toward her. I trusted her about as much as I could throw her.

I pretended to "like" my boss when she tried to be friends. She is a person who backstabs, gossips, is very negative and was just truly was and is toxic to me. I would be under her until I took things into my own hands and demanded a supervisor change.

LOVE BITES

During my stint at the charter school, I was working at Herbergers (Department Store) as a second job. On one horrible day, I received a call from a guy who claimed we had communicated on a dating site. I hadn't been on the site for quite some time so I was somewhat surprised.

He asked me if I could meet him for coffee as at the time we were communicating it was not a good time for him. I didn't really want to meet as I was tired of the dating scene. Unfortunately, I made the bad decision to meet him for coffee.

Well, to my surprise, he really liked me and we would see each other again. I would let him use my car as he did not have one, and was from a foreign country. He was basically using me. Yet again, a scene that played out over and over again in my life.

Over the course of that year he would stay with me at my apartment and we would fight a lot and make up. I would miss several red flags over that year and consequently, during our marriage. He was a narcissist, emotionally and mentally abusive to me and would lie and steal more than money from me.

One summer day in May, he asked me to marry him and made all these promises to work hard, and that we'd have a great future together full of roses, lolly pops, glitter and unicorns. Instead, I ended up in hell.

He said he wanted to work, and I honestly thought that he loved me. At the time, I loved him as well. He painted a future that looked amazing that consequently would never happen.

Unfortunately, I believed him and we were married the following December. Biggest. Regret. Ever. I wish everyday that I had told him no and walked away from the relationship. However, I was 38, lonely and didn't really know what love was or even what a healthy relationship was at that time as I had never seen one.

Life with him would be one catastrophe after another. He wouldn't ever have money so I was constantly paying for everything. He would borrow money from me and not pay it back.

I would have to pay all the bills, sacrifice my car, help him find jobs that he would simply quit after a month or two. The gaslighting, the lack of seeing me as his partner and the abuse would continue for 7 long years. The disrespect was so blatant.

I was getting older and when you are lost and desperate, you don't make the best decisions. I regret it to this day. I deserved so much better but I didn't know my worth. ALWAYS…ALWAYS KNOW. YOUR. WORTH.

I had grown up in a family that didn't seem to value me. I was always getting yelled at by my dad and being called a "dub" a "pest" or a "brat." Those things wear on you. When you are called those things continuously you begin to believe it as being true.

My mother was also such a mess that I had no idea what or how I was supposed to approach a relationship as my parents' marriage was so toxic and my upbringing was so traumatic. My mother loved the dogs more than her kids and my dad favored my sister. It's no wonder I felt so worthless as a human being.

Resilience wasn't a thing in my life, aversion to adversity wasn't even considered. I thought that life was simply misery and things would never change. For most of my life, it was that way.

Thing is, I had to deal with the trauma and learn these things as an adult which is really difficult. These lessons are usually learned in school through having love relationships and friendships. It took a very long time to learn these lessons, but once I learned them, I never looked back.

My parents were a mess. Their marriage was toxic. Growing up I had seen and known no different. I didn't have anything but friendship relationships in high school or college. I had dated but I was such a mess that I didn't attract the attention of the best people and thus, I never had a full fledged love relationship up until that point.

I thought I was unlovable and truly felt that way. I thought I was ugly and just worthless for so long. He came along and told me I was "beautiful" and his "queen." My ex claimed he "loved" me and that was all I needed.

What I didn't know is that actions speak louder than words. Love is not pain. He loved that he could live off of and manipulate me. I paid rent, food, insurance, cell phone bills, hospital bills among many other things.

He did go to trucking school to be a semi driver. He finished and started at a company but the job only lasted about 6 months. He would work for 3 trucking companies and hold a job with each of them for only 2-3 months. He told me that he simply couldn't work under someone. So, he decided to do Uber.

I let him use my car for Uber, he wanted an SUV as my car didn't earn him enough money so he pestered me to no end to get a car loan for him. I stupidly did. That used car had so many issues and gas was so expensive that he complained again about not making enough money. He wanted my car again.

Now, I was stuck with an SUV I hated, a car payment I didn't need and I was trapped in a marriage with someone I no longer loved who was a financial catastrophe and a huge financial burden.

Our marriage would last just short of 8 years. During those years, I never got Christmas presents, though I gave him gifts that he refused to wear or simply broke. He never remembered my birthday and I finally just stopped telling him when the day rolled around.

I celebrated it with my parents. I always remembered his birthday and I also gave him nice gifts when I got nothing. He never asked when my birthday was. I don't think he cared. I remember the birthdays of the people who mean the most to me. I think it's important to acknowledge their special day. Sadly, he didn't think the way I did.

I did not receive gifts for much of anything or for our anniversary though I would give him things he simply didn't respect or take care of. I did get a rose that died a day later for Valentine's Day. Needless to say, it made me hate the Hallmark holiday even more.

It was so painful. I did love him and I tried to "prove" it but everything I gave him was meaningless. Much like my parents, sister and many more in my life at that time, he only took and never gave. My well ran so dry. I had nothing left at that time. I was a "thing" or an "it" yet again. To him, I had no feelings and basically was his puppet or someone who simply paid the bills.

I bought him a $2000 computer which he "accidentally" threw out in the trash. He didn't even bother to try to track it down or do anything about it. It was just as meaningless as I was to him.

He claimed to actually "love" me but his actions spoke louder than his words. He would often tell me how lucky I was to have him because he could have any woman he wanted. Funny. I didn't feel all that lucky.

He would make me cry and tell me simply that he didn't care.

He said it was my job to be "intimate" with him. On more than one occasion it hurt and I yelled out that he was hurting me and to stop. He didn't stop. It hurt a lot and he also went in the "backdoor" without my permission on more than one occasion.

I would bleed and hurt for days. I would tell him I didn't like it and he would do it anyway. I have yet to have an enjoyable intimate experience. I still cannot watch movies with nudity as it makes my stomach turn.

From that point on, all I wanted was a divorce and to get out relatively painlessly. I would start talking to lawyers in 2018. I was trying to make it work, so at that time, I didn't pursue divorce. I really, really wish I had as the narcissistic abuse would get worse and worse over the years we were married.

When we were dating he would want me to bring him my car so he could go to church or some other reason. I would bring it over and he wouldn't bring it back when I requested. He would leave me alone in the apartment for hours on end without the ability to take care of things I needed to take care of.

I would be yelling at him and telling him I wanted the car as I had places to go but he simply couldn't be bothered by my needs. That was our marriage, totally and completely about his needs and his needs only. I was simply an afterthought.

One day in October of 2022, he called and said he had something to tell me and that I couldn't freak out. I thought maybe he had been in a car accident or something like that. That is easily fixable. Painful, but as long as he was okay.

He told me he had a 3 year old daughter. I was so confused as we didn't have any children and then it occurred to me that he had been having an affair. He had called the police on the child's mother for some reason. He wanted me to "cover" for him. I was physically sick and told him I would call him the next day which I had no intention of doing.

Instead, I went to work absolutely dying inside. I cried non-stop at work when my boss was not around. It was gut-wrenching, agonizing, and horribly painful. I was so hurt. I wrote to my doctor via Mychart and told him what had happened.

I made an appointment with my doctor and he recommended a divorce. I was scared I'd lose everything and I was still hurt and unsure. I thought maybe we could try to work it out. I called around for a marriage counselor. I knew if we were to get through this, we would need professional help. It was simply too big of an issue to try to get over by myself.

He would not hear of this and said that he would not go to counseling because it wouldn't change me. For some reason this was my fault. I would see him one last time in November where his daughters toys, clothes etc. would be out and it would be like a knife stabbed through my heart.

I knew it wasn't her fault. If anything, she and I were innocent in this but she was a reminder of the betrayal. It was simply too difficult to see those things, so I told him I needed some time to be away from him. It was simply too painful.

He would go back to Liberia that January and not contact me except for 1 email. I went and got international calls on my cell phone to call so we could talk. I called the first time and he hung up on me. The second and third tries, he did the same thing.

I tried calling on a different day and he answered. For some reason he didn't recognize my number or my voice. I've had the same number for over 20 years. I thought this was quite strange.

When he finally figured out it was me, he told me that he had a butler, driver and maid in Liberia and that he was doing really well. He was also not living with his dad. I had my suspicions that he was living with another woman.

Though he refused to work for people, he had this idea that he was somehow going to become a multi-millionaire. It's been over 9 years since he told me this and he's still not a multi millionaire. What a surprise!

He had all these ideas for inventions but he could never afford the patent or wanted me to do research on how to get a patent. I did this all without being paid and on top of working and going to school.

I had started a Public Health Degree at the University. I again, wasted money on getting a degree I simply would come to believe wasn't worth all the work and I didn't agree with all the theories and train of thought of the degree.

I would get the patent information and give it to him. He wouldn't do anything with it. He just simply wanted me to do all the work which I wasn't willing to do. This was another ongoing thing in our relationship. I would do all the work and he would simply sit back and watch.

On Easter of 2023, I was sitting in church ashamed and feeling unworthy as I hadn't been there for so long. While listening to the sermon, this voice came to me either God or my intuition saying "get the negative out of your life." I knew exactly what that voice meant. It meant to divorce my horrible husband, get my horrible boss out of my life and to cut ties with my mother. I would do two out of the three that summer.

That night I wrote my soon to be ex a "Dear John" letter telling him that I wanted a divorce. I mentioned all the horrible things he had done to me to which he said I was lying about. He said the things I mentioned in the letter never happened. It was his typical way of gaslighting me.

He could never admit all the abusive things he had done to me. It was always me and my actions that were at fault. Nothing was ever his fault. In his eyes, he walked on water. He was a typical narcissist.

He would blame me for depending too much on my parents. Truth be told, I couldn't depend on him for anything. He never kept his promises, would make decisions without consulting me, and go out with other women without telling me.

I started to do the same and it made him mad. He never had money and I had to pay all the bills. Sad as it was, my parents were the only people I could depend on at that time.

In April of 2023 I would contact our HR Rep asking for a few different things. I had been asking for a different boss. I knew that if I was to get through the divorce I would need support as I just couldn't tell my parents what I was going through. I never told them that I had gotten married. They really didn't like him and he wanted to keep it a secret until he could tell his family. I felt so ashamed living a lie. It was stressful, shameful and I just ended up wanting to divorce him.

I still haven't told my family I was married. They would and will probably judge me harshly and hang me out to dry. At least I was able to get out of the relationship relatively easily and quickly.

I had talked to my Director about changing bosses earlier that year but he wanted to wait to see if things improved. Consequently, they didn't. My boss kept abusing power and dumping work on me. I was burning out every one to two months.

I emailed our HR rep to set up a meeting and sobbed as I told her what had happened with my marriage, the abuse and how my boss was abusing power. She said she would see what she could do and talk to my Director. I also had emailed the Director of Graduate Studies who I had wanted to be my new boss.

I told him everything. I had forgot he was a mandated reporter, so due to the times of forced "intimacy" that were against my permission, he had to report that I had been raped. I was contacted by various centers at the University and they recommended the Aurora Center. They recommended a center for women outside of the University.

At that agency I talked with a lawyer who recommended affordable divorce lawyers. My lawyer was phenomenal. I couldn't afford the retainer right away. My ex returned from Libera and gave me back my car as he no longer needed it.

It needed $3000 of repairs. Again, since it was mine, he abused it and didn't take care of it. I fixed and sold the car to afford my lawyer's retainer. I hated the SUV I had the car loan on. He didn't want it and my name was on it, so I had traded it in for a smaller, new car.

I was upside down in the loan but at least I was grateful that I could afford the payment. Lesson learned to never ever sign a loan for someone else unless you both are responsible for it. Make sure that person is trustworthy and actually is willing to make the payments as well. He didn't have good credit. I had to sign and only my name was on the loan so I was stuck with it.

He would get nothing in the divorce as he could not afford a lawyer or simply didn't want to fight for anything. It was truly a blessing for me. I thought it was going to be a horrible experience. It could have been so much worse and I'm so grateful that it was an easy process. It was a matter of signing papers and moving on which I did. I told him that I wished him well but that I needed to move on with my life and that he needed to do the same.

I also didn't want to ruin his daughter's life. I didn't think I could get past the betrayal. It was in no way her fault, but without counseling and dealing with the anger, I knew it wouldn't be fair to her. Divorce was the only and best option for her and I.

FREEDOM

My divorce was finalized in July of 2023. I would work on finding out why I ended up marrying someone like him. I'm grateful today for my divorce lawyer and for an easy, almost painless divorce. My ex walked out with nothing of mine. I was truly blessed and someone was looking out for me.

I would spend time alone reflecting and reading books on narcissistic abuse and figuring out what to look for in relationships, changing my behavior, outlook and learning to love myself. I didn't want this to happen again and I surely didn't want to rush into another relationship and have the same results. I waited until I encountered a server at a restaurant I liked going to who would change my life for the better.

Thankfully, I didn't have to pay alimony or give my ex part of my retirement. I'm so grateful to be free of him and his abuse. I had to meet him to take care of a financial transaction last March.

I told him the bank where I would be and he was over an hour late. I almost left when I saw him. He couldn't understand why I was upset. This was the story of our marriage. I would wait and he may or may not show. If he did show, it was 45-60 minutes after we agreed to meet.

We took care of the transaction and I started to leave. He stopped me and told me he wanted to talk to me. I made the mistake of stopping and he proceeded to tell me that we didn't need to get divorced?

He said that it was because of my emotions why things didn't work out which was a lie. He was blameless in his eyes. He also told me he still "loved" me. I felt something was off. But he wanted to meet for coffee to "talk."

I told him I would text him that weekend but when I arrived home I talked with my besties and they told me I felt off because he gaslighted me. I'm so glad I checked with them. It's always good to have friends who have your back. I didn't always have that.

Thankfully, I didn't meet him and I've blocked him again from my phone. I worked the day he wanted to meet and he texted and asked me why I didn't text him to go for coffee. I told him I was too tired and simply didn't want to talk to him.

He didn't contact me again until Easter of 2024 to which I again blocked him on my phone and deleted his message. I hope to be rid of him forever and for him to never contact me again. He can have any woman he wants but he will NEVER EVER again have me.

I learned that narcissists are attracted to empaths. I can feel people's emotions. I know what they are feeling as I have been able to do this since I was young. It's usually due to early childhood trauma.

I found out when reading about empaths that I am one. My Meyers-Briggs personality is INFJ which is the rarest personality type and the type of most empaths. I know the jury is still out on empaths, but I strongly believe I am one.

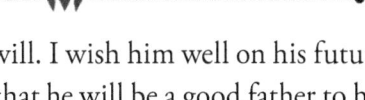

I don't wish my ex ill will. I wish him well on his future endeavors and I hope that he will be a good father to his daughter. That doesn't mean I ever want to see him or have anything to do with him.

The scar is healed but it is still there. I now know what to look for and how to see the "red flags." I've grown a lot since marrying and divorcing him. I've become a person I respect and I know my worth. That other woman is gone. I'm still a work-in-progress but I work on who I am everyday. Everyday I learn something new.

MOVING ON

I would spend the next year falling for another guy, reading up on various things like goals and life dreams. I would spend more time with my friends and begin to heal from my ordeal. I would also spend more time with my sister. The shame and humiliation of living a lie was over. I was free.

My parents and I would go to a certain local restaurant on occasion. I didn't know many people there but on this occasion it was really busy. My mom being the impatient person she is, couldn't wait for our order to be taken and was really rude to a server. I took one look at him and I was smitten. I told my mother she had been rude and she threatened to punch me in the mouth, and kick me out of the house twice.

Mom also consequently told me that I couldn't be friends with a pharmacist from where I worked as a pharmacy technician. This woman attended our church. My mom didn't like her. To which, I told her it was my choice to be friends with this person.

She became more and more angry and agitated. I would spend most of my time that night back at the restaurant eating cake and trying to figure out what to do. I spent it talking with the server. He was so handsome, funny and way out of my league. He was so amazing.

I would spend the holiday season thinking about him and going to the restaurant. I was so awkward and I didn't know how to act without looking stupid or weird though I ended up looking like both. He would end up disliking me…for a while.

He was really upset at something where he simply seemed so angry when I tried to talk to him. One day I went and made him laugh and we were good. I managed to ask him out but he told me his "lady" would "get mad." He is the only guy I ever had the courage to ask out on a date. I was so nervous but he was really, really sweet about it.

I kept going and he would go out with his S/O for dinner and Valentine's Day but didn't seem happy. I asked him if he was happy and he told me very unconvincingly that he was happy. I didn't believe him as the pain showing in his eyes and in his voice was so raw and real.

My parents would leave for Arizona that March and I didn't know how to cook so I simply went to the restaurant. I didn't expect it, but I was always seated in his section. He would do amazing things for me like get my order ahead of other people who had been there longer and sit and talk to me if he wasn't busy.

He'd tell me things about his life and remember small details of things I told him. I overheard him call me "my girl "on several occasions. We just seemed to have a real connection and I developed feelings for him that I still have.

He is amazing but in a relationship where he is so unhappy. He has a son with this S/O and kids from his previous marriage. His S/O has several issues. I know he wants out but doesn't quite know how. I aimed to teach him his worth as he deserves so much better. Would I give anything to be with him? Yes! However, I care about him so much that even if he didn't/doesn't choose me, I just want him to be happy in life.

His S/O simply has no idea what she has in him. I would take him in a second and never let him go unless he wanted. Even if we don't end up together (I'm still going), I just want him to be free of the misery and to be happy.

He was married for 20 years and divorced. I'm thinking that maybe he didn't wait a year before dating again and found this woman. Like me, when you're lost, lonely and hurting, you don't make the best decisions.

When the crosses are extremely heavy and you're hauling them up Killamonjaros sometimes it makes it easier when you have someone to help you bear the weight. Totally been there. But to a narcissist that is an opportunity to show up and be and do horrible things.

He is amazing and I would be honored to be with him. Frankly, eternity wouldn't be long enough. To quote Lisa Kudro in one of her commencement addresses, "he's so way out of my league." I'm so lucky to have met him. I'd be even more grateful to be with him.

Now, I will not destroy a relationship. I keep things platonic. I know he has feelings for me as I do for him. However I will not help him cheat-not that he would. This is because if he were willing to cheat with me, he'd more than likely be willing to cheat on me. The whole trust thing. I also will not destroy an existing relationship.

He's unhappy. He needs to make choices. I cannot make those choices for him. I wouldn't want to. He deserves to be free and happy. Whether that is with the woman he's with, with me or with someone totally different. He needs to realize his worth and realize that he's worth so much more than what he's getting right now.

WHAT I'VE LEARNED

Life is going to always be difficult. As I have gotten older, life has just become more challenging. I consider it growth. Growth is difficult but it makes you stronger as a person. That is what has happened to me. I don't have control over the guy I hope to one day have or when or how things happen to me. I do have control over how I react.

I used to think that wasn't power, however it is incredible power. Having power or control over other people is not something I ever want and is almost impossible. If it were possible, it's too much responsibility.

People will show their true colors eventually. I've learned that people can hurt you so deeply and they can be the people you would least expect. Trust is built, respect is given. I respect my parents, however I will never trust them.

My mother can be so mean when she's wrathful and will say mean things, lie and backstab. I love them and my sister from afar. I have been hurt by people who I thought were my friends and turned out to be different behind closed doors.

Authentic people are difficult to find. My friend circle has shrunk as I fully trust fewer and fewer people as I've gotten older. I've just learned that trust is important and

I need to know I can trust the people I have in my life. That my friends are the people who they are in front of me and behind closed doors. I'm the same person out in society and behind closed doors.

I defend my friends when they are not around. I expect the same from them. No less. If I care about you, I show it. If they don't give back in some way, I will eventually cut them free. Love and friendship are both a two-way street. I don't give unconditionally anymore. I give to those who give back.

I don't do social media, I don't like going to bars or parties. I hate weddings, funerals, baby showers, birthday parties and wedding showers. I like small, intimate gatherings with 2-4 people.

I want little to do with my extended family and they are all married and have kids of their own. They did nothing to alleviate my suffering and they knew what was going on. I have my reasons, and I just don't want contact with them. I consider myself the "black sheep" of the family. I've always been different.

I was always a square peg in a round hole. I will forever be different and that I've learned is okay. Everyone loves my sister. Different as I am, I have found friends and a certain server who appreciates my uniqueness.

I don't have time for BS. Time is precious and I want to spend time with those who matter most to me, my friends, and eventually, maybe a certain server. I know they stand up for me and will always have my back.

Life is not linear, it is backwards, down, left, right and a mess of everything in between. I used to think life was a straight line. I used to compare myself to my sister and wonder why my life wasn't where I wanted it to be. It made me really miserable. I now know her life isn't perfect. That sometimes she's a hot mess. Comparison is the thief of happiness.

I will, one day soon, have the life I've always wanted. Living with my parents isn't where I want my life to be but it is where I am right now. I want to get married, maybe have children and live the rest of my life with my spouse.

Once I find him, or if I've already found him, I don't want to live another day without him. I've spent 46 years looking for him. That's a long time, and though I wasn't ready and made many mistakes along the way, the wait will be or was worth it to find him.

Again, as I mentioned, I am not a victim. I will NEVER be a victim. A victim has no power. I'm a survivor. Too many people in this world play the "victim card." I had choices in my life and I decided to make my circumstances different. I dealt with the pain. I realized things could be different, and I wanted to change.

For the future, my spouse and my kids, I want a different life. I do not want to pass the dysfunction, pain, resentment, feelings of worthlessness and anger onto them. I want happiness, love and a healthy, loving marriage. I want the children I have or any children my spouse has to know that they are loved and valued.

We have choices in life and we make choices that affect our lives. No one makes those choices for us. I wanted to get better so I put myself through therapy. My parents and my sister did things they should not have done which caused me a ton of trauma.

However, they more than likely have been traumatized in life. My mother lost her parents at a young age. Her oldest brother did horrible things to my maternal grandmother because the guy is an epic, epic asshole. The woman (Grandma) lost her husband and had to raise her kids by herself in the 1950's. She suffered immensely and lived to die. Living in that house probably wasn't paradise.

Lord knows a 16 year-old at the time, who was such an epic asshole, who thinks he's the shit must have been hell. Lord knows he's aptly named. He has the same name as the male doll in a certain horror flick that causes horror and terror in his victims.

But that is just the movies. Uncle Dearest caused an epic amount of pain for his mother and siblings so much that they would have to call her brother, Boom, over to put him in his place. I really wish I could have met her, but she died before I was born. To my asshole, oldest uncle on my mom's side; be a man and face what you did.

You're a coward, a liar and SO full of SHIT! I hope you're really proud of the man you are and what you did. Your siblings think you're a joke and so do I. One sister would feed you cyanide if you were stupid enough to take it. That's a lot of hate. Then again, I now understand why.

My paternal grandfather was an alcoholic. Life wasn't' roses for either of my parents. However, they had choices and made choices in life to carry that trauma and pass it onto my sister and I.

Do I hate them? No, I think they have made choices in their lives that were not the best. My dad should have divorced my mother a long time ago, but his house and money mattered more than happiness. I have to say that I would have made a different decision.

Cheating is the one thing I will not tolerate in my relationship. Trust, once broken, is never the same again. I simply can't be with a cheater. I respect myself too much to ever stay with someone who does that.

Simply, if you are not happy in your marriage, just leave. Divorce sucks! I totally know. But sometimes blowing up what is existing and starting new is necessary and a much better option. Painful? Yes, but it is worth having a life worth living.

Mom wanted to leave with the last guy she had an affair with. Mom was such a prize that he decided to stay with his wife so she didn't leave. I really wish she had gone. We obviously meant nothing to her but she stayed and caused a ton more trauma instead. A divorce was welcome at that time, and still is. It will never happen and that is my father's choice.

I told my father not long ago that he could have saved us a ton of pain if he had only divorced her and sent her on her merry way. He didn't, and the consequences were devastating. Pain, ruined milestones, vacations, holidays and special occasions were the result of letting her stay.

It was meant to hurt because it's the truth. Both of my parents and sister have caused me enormous amounts of pain in my life and I'm walking and loving them from afar for my protection. But I do not hate them!

Hate only hurts the person with the anger, resentment and pain. If I hate them, it gives them power. They've had so much power over me in my life that I don't want to give them anymore. I have forgiven them. Forgiveness is for the one doing the forgiving. Not for those who have caused the pain.

Hate eats people and causes nothing but problems. It's a vicious cycle that is neverending. I don't want that pain/anger cycle in my life. I want peace and love. Hate does not offer that. It only offers pain and darkness.

Do I have moments when I wish things were different... yes. I wish I could be best friends with my mom. That she could go back to being the mom of my early years. That we could go shopping, out to lunch and I could share my life with her.

I don't tell her much about my life because she makes everything about her and her wants and needs. She will never be the mom I needed or wanted. That woman is gone...forever.

I wish I had love and support from my dad. I wish he was giving and loved me the same as he loves my sister. That he would give more than take. He will not give money, gifts etc. unless I agree to pay him back. I have brought both of them out to dinner, bought coffee and tried to be a good daughter.

However the free rent seemed to be something, in fact, that no matter what I gave in return was not enough. The free rent in a house they both owned, to respect my privacy, not go batshit crazy and threaten to kick me out and punch me in the mouth for sticking up for what is right-defending the server I care so much about is her right because I didn't pay rent. The "Free Rent" is just not worth the pain. Fuck you, mommy!

I would do it 10 billion times the national debt, again. Needless to say, I was able to get a nice raise and now I can afford to walk and walk I will do. I was able to get into a beautiful building built in 2023. I absolutely love my new place. It's small, but it is perfect for now.

I have met one man who gives back and I fell for him. The server. He actually gives back and I give to him. He seems to understand my love language. I've never had a man who actually gave back. It's so nice and feels amazing.

All the men in my life up to this point have only taken and haven't given back. My ex is a really good example. He sucked me and my well dry. I had nothing left when I was going through divorce because he had simply drained me, emotionally, mentally and physically. A good reason to always take care of yourself first. Put your own oxygen mask on first.

I didn't get to choose my family but I do get to choose my spouse and my friends. I have made mistakes in the people I've chosen. I can't change the past. It's already done and gone. There is no such thing as a Delorean time machine so there's no going back to fix or change things. I have power over the present and I can choose for a better future for myself.

Everyone has the power to change the present and to better themselves. I take the opportunity to do that every day. Everyday I try to make myself better than the day before.

Again, I have choices. We all do. I have to play the cards I've been dealt and make the best life decisions for me. I have to make the painful decision to cut my parents and my sister-she needs to learn to respect me and know who I am, out of my life.

My sister thinks I'm broken. She is soooo wrong. I was never broken, I simply got lost in life. It happens when the two people who were supposed to protect and love you do a horrible job of raising you.

When there is not enough love in a household, the kids fight over it. Thing is, in our household, I let my sister win and I took the hit. My sister is so judgemental, assumes too many things and likes to criticize people for the decisions they make-including me.

Far be it that she actually believes that I suffered or gave up anything such as the tiny bit of love our horribly messed up parents could give. I just loved her so much. All I wanted was to be best friends with my sister but she was so insistent on hating me when we were young. Lord knows! She could be so mean.

Anyway, if life gives me lemons, I have the choice to use the lemons to my advantage or simply waste them. We all do.

Solving the problems or the issue at hand is what is important. Crying and feeling sorry for myself is not an option. That's what a victim does and I am NOT and NEVER will be or act like a victim. Things are not always about me. I didn't know about resiliency and getting back on the right track until much later in life, but at least I learned the lesson. Late is better than never.

Life is indeed pain. Confucius (Buddah) was so right. If there is one thing we as humans despise, try to bury and avoid, it's pain. But that doesn't make the pain go away. It just makes the pain worse.

Alcohol, drugs, being abusive, making people hurt because you do is a really terrible, shitty option. Thankfully, I went "inside" instead of doing those things. Something in me just couldn't hurt anyone or abuse my body. Somehow, someone in this household showed me the consequences of those things for most of my life.

As for trauma, we are all responsible for healing our trauma. There simply just is not enough money in the world to pay for all the trauma caused hundreds of years ago up until now. Lord knows, you should punish people for something that happened 100's of years ago. Those people are long, cold and dead in their coffins.

WHEN BAD PEOPLE DO HORRIBLE THINGS

Holding someone up as a hero when they've been in prison for threatening to kill a pregnant woman's baby, had five or so kids from 5 different women-none of whom he married; was a drug addict and had like 15-18 finances is, frankly, crazy. Questions like did he have a job, was he paying child support and was he actually in the lives of his 5 kids? Those kinds of questions were never raised. Was he a good dad to all of his kids. All these questions were NEVER brought up.

Burning a city and protesting on a highway, stopping traffic is also just INSANE! Then again, just because you believe that your cause should disrupt people's lives so much that you need to burn a city, protest and ruin graduation ceremonies all in the name of your cause. That is so SELFISH!

Give me a peaceful protest, bring people together and have a conversation, maybe over coffee. Try peace. Try love. Try understanding. Try anything but destruction and devastation. Come on! Do better!

Some things that people do all in the name of their cause is very sickening. Just this year, not even 3 weeks ago, Students for Democracy (a student group for the Palestinian cause) at the University, entered the Administration building (the Presidents' office is there) with scarves over their faces (like terrorists), blocked entrance to doors, sprayed black paint over security cameras and basically held the employees hostage. They would not let the employees leave all in the name of THEIR cause.

That is so epically wrong and very, very selfish on so many levels. It angers me so much. That could have been my department or a department where I have friends. They did so much destruction and damage that the Administrative building is now closed and has to be fixed.

They also made a huge mess in the Coffman Memorial Union. Those students should be ASHAMED of themselves. They terrorized those employees. They are an embarrassment to the university and should be expelled and forced to pay for the damage and destruction they caused.

They were arrested but certain groups-frankly pathetic people-have posted their bail all in the name of free speech. If you cause destruction, terrorize employees, hold them hostage, you should be punished and not bailed out of jail.

That is not "free speech," that is terrorism. I hope the judge in all their cases gives the maximum punishment for these students. There was no excuse for what they did. They went way too far.

I get you have a cause but if you protest on roads stopping traffic, camp on college campuses where you make a huge mess and cause destruction, burn a city and hold people (employees) hostage, I will NEVER support your cause no matter what. I don't like people that do horrible things all in the name of what THEY believe. That's so horrible and selfish to say the least.

You want to peacefully protest, that's fine but going as far as to terrorize employees is just something I cannot support. Find a better way like Ghandi or Martin Luther King. Those two got it right.

Maybe we should try their way. We need more people like those two brave men who were killed for basically standing up for what they believed. They saw a better world and found a better way. It's much harder but the rewards it reaps are endless. It's so much better than terror and destruction but it is a much harder, longer road as history will explain.

A great senator back in the early 2000's once said "We all do better when we all do better." I miss that senator. Paul Wellstone was amazing. He died in a plane crash in 2002 along with some of his campaign people and his wife. That guy was epic. He could bring the two parties together. Miss that guy. We need more people like him.

I would ask that woman and her child what they think of that "hero" who died at the hands of police in Minneapolis on Memorial Day weekend. The city burned, people lost businesses and the military had to be called in for goodness sakes.

I'm sure that mom and her child would have something to say about him. Needless to say, the media is probably too scared to even try but then they lie and are full of shit. They just want to sensationalize and get ratings. Fuck the truth!

Just the fact that the guy was African American and the officer was caucasian screams racism. There really isn't any proof but frankly, I don't care. Villainizing police making a department pay so much for the actions of a few bad apples doesn't really make sense.

Making stupid laws that make life hard for officers has caused the Minneapolis police to lose many officers. They can't even recruit officers. They are down 400 officers. No one wants to work for the Minneapolis police. I can't blame them.

They've been vilified. Who wants to work for an employer where you can be prosecuted and thrown into jail for a split second decision. Police have to make those decisions on a wim, everyday. It's just not worth it.

The City Counsel, who frankly all the members on it couldn't equal a quarter of a human brain, have made it especially difficult. Gosh! They have made some epically horrible, horrible decisions.

Frankly, I won't even drive into the city or even THINK of living in it due to the shitty decisions the council and the mayor have made. The Mayor isn't any better. Frankly, I'm not sure why people keep voting for him because he's so terrible.

In my opinion, if I were to run the country, politicians would not get paid, football players would make minimum wage and simply play for the love of the game. CEO's would also make very little money so those who actually do the work could actually get paid their worth. They are priceless and work so hard and get so little money for it.

US AND STATE GOVERNMENT STUPIDITY AND RIDICULOUSNESS

Lord knows in the election that was a couple of weeks ago, we elected Satan. It was basically a tossup between Satan and the Grim reaper. Either way we were going to Hell. It was just a matter of who was taking us. Neither one of the two candidates was close to qualified in any way.

One candidate, the Vice President, wanted to give out money to everyone, spend, spend, spend. And didn't do anything significant while in office. She would only talk about her family, how she grew up…blah…blah…blah.

Lord knows her running mate has cost Minnesota huge amounts of money. He and the genius democratic led legislature made pot legal, made it so the state insurance plan for the poor would cover illegal immigrants, made school lunches free for everyone. Minneapolis is a sanctuary city, I'm disappointed to say. Again, if people are here illegally, they should not be here or have cities that protect them.

Evidently, these "special" government officials think that money just falls from the sky. They can just spend, spend, spend on ridiculous things. I'm seriously tired of paying and I bet that 99.9 percent of the Minnesota population is too.

Our outstanding state government officials are also giving the state Tribes sports betting and a few years of supplying the pot to the idiots that smoke it. Also, the only "casino-like" entity that is owned by the state the Native Americans want to close. They are coming close.

We couldn't use the money that is generated as a result of sports betting. The office that does the projecting projected wrong yet again and things cost more than anticipated. Minnesota's genius politicians had to cover a deficit the last legislative session for which they again hit up the taxpayers with an increase in sales tax.

Here's the thing. I absolutely hate the smell of pot. There is no way to test if someone is driving high. The police actually have to see the pot in the hands of the driver. Unfortunately, people do stupid things and drive high.

Someone, high on pot probably one day soon, will probably kill or seriously injure someone. Since we have no way of testing to see if someone is high, that horrible person, who got behind the wheel will not be held responsible for killing another human being. Sad!

There is no mention on how to fix the real problems in the country like wasting money on foreign aid, cutting taxes that are simply too high, closing loopholes that allow billionaires and the super rich to have "shell" companies, hold their money in an offshore account or a Swiss bank account to prevent the IRS from seeing it. These people NEED to start paying up. I have to pay my taxes and so should billionaires.

Imagine the money that we could have if those individuals and corporations actually PAID their taxes.

Maybe student loans could be forgiven. Heck, maybe college tuition could be made cheaper, maybe, just maybe, those lower on the totem pole could have their tax burden cut. Oh my Gosh! That makes sense.

Ya see the government has cut positions in the IRS so there simply isn't enough staff to go after those who are not paying their fair share of taxes. Again, imagine the money that would be going through and actually paying off the national debt as it was paid off in the 1990's.

We need to solve the problem at the Mexican border. If someone is here illegally, they cannot stay. We as a country are not a charity. We cannot take up all of the world's suffering. There simply aren't enough resources.

Perhaps Europe could take some of these immigrants. They don't want to because they are socialist societies that actually pay for their citizens and enact good laws to protect them. Their taxpayers also do not want to pay for the cost of immigrants. It would be too costly for their system as it is too costly for ours as well.

These "illegal immigrants" need to play the cards they were given and make changes to their country's government. The US taxpayers are SO TIRED of paying for things that are simply too expensive and wasteful.

These "illegals" steal someone's identity which is sooo unacceptable. The immigrant uses the victims social security number to be able to work. Frankly, that creates a huge nightmare for the person whose identity was stolen.

I know our immigration system is broken but the only way someone should get into the country is through that broken system. It's unfair but we simply don't have the money or the resources at this point.

Well, I really wish that the current Vice President and everyone else in congress, senate and legislatures would simply talk to an economics professor or someone who could explain that giving out free money to every man, woman and child actually causes inflation in the long term.

They are just more interested in kicking the can down the road. Sort of like they do with Social Security. The Boomer generation is sucking it dry. They actually vote more than the other 3 generations. Politicians are up for reelection every so often, and need the votes. Money is a great thing and the posh apartment in Washington DC is really nice. Unfortunately, those things seem to cloud the fact that we simply cannot afford to keep paying Social Security and Medicare at its current rate.

Both systems need to be cut if it is to be available for the next generations. Unfortunately, none of the cowards, money-sucking, crooked, greedy politicians want to be voted out or stand up for what is morally right.

I believe the Social Security system will be bankrupt by 2030 or 2035. The Boomer generation (the largest generation to date) has this idea that they are entitled to social security as they paid into it.

I'm also currently paying into it and I will probably not get it when I retire. I have a good head on my shoulders so I'm planning with a 401K and a 401B which the

Boomers just trusted the government would take care of them. Huge mistake!

They were SO wrong! The government spent their money on two waste of time wars to find and kill a terrorist they actually trained. No wonder the guy was so hard to find. He was trained by the US government to do horrible things.

Unfortunately, he turned, got really, really pissed off at the US and recruited people to drive 2 planes into the World Trade Center and have one crash into the Pentagon. The last plane didn't make it to the White House, thankfully. It crashed in a field killing all aboard.

We lost 1000's. It didn't need to happen. Place blame where it belongs; on the US government. They make such horrible, horrible decisions. Perhaps the politicians who make these horrible decisions can pay the Boomers social security out of their own pockets. After all, they made the shitty decisions that caused so many families to lose their loved ones basically for no reason.

I really wish I could take the money I'm paying into social security and invest it. I would make so much more money in the end. It's such a waste of money that I have to pay for a Boomer and I won't even get it when I retire.

They are somewhat greedy, and waste the money at the casino. Evidently, if you can waste $1000's at the casino, you really don't need the money as you are giving it away on a very minute chance of winning. What a waste!

Well, with social security you pay in all your life but at retirement you are sucking at least 5-10 times what you paid into it. That is some messed up system. No wonder it's such a mess. On top of that, we have people sucking from it who haven't worked all their lives and take advantage of the system to get disability.

A former friend of mine who was from one of the camps in Thailand came over with her family. Her mother didn't want to or for some reason couldn't learn English so she was able to get disability. She had 3 kids though her husband divorced her. One night her ex husband showed back up, she let him in and got pregnant with the third child. The ass didn't pay child support so the mom went to get welfare and also ended up getting social security. So utterly ridiculous.

MY TAKE ON THINGS

Lord knows politicians are swayed by big donors like corporations, drug companies, insurance companies, tobacco companies. Far be it for them to do what's right for the people who actually voted them into office.

Gosh! When shit really hits the fan and they are supposed to go back to their state to explain their logic in voting for such evil corporations; they don't want to face the voters. The very people who put them into office in the first place. They are such COWARDS!

Lord knows, I'm thankful for the police. We need law and order as a society. There is chaos if you don't have that. Thank God there are people who do that job with dignity and respect. Those people are my heroes. I have many like nurses, firefighters, those in the military, 911 operators, healthcare workers, servers, coffee house workers, janitors, road construction workers and many many more. Too many to list. I am so grateful for all they do. Lord knows they aren't given enough credit or thanks for what they do.

The fact is we are human. Police are, believe it or not, human. They have an epically shitty job and frankly everyone has their breaking point. It's sad that a man had to die for that but maybe on that warm, summer MEMORIAL DAY, that cop just got really, epically fed up with a man who two other cops could not get under control.

He just fucking wouldn't sit in the back of a cop car. He just was so out of control because he was high on drugs. God help us! One officer offered to sit with him in the car. That officer is sitting in jail along with his partner who had been on the force for less than a month. Lord knows you know how to do everything on a job that just has an epically large amount of stuff to learn in less than a month.

Frankly, in policing, one could lose their life to some piece of shit person with a gun. But, a man who was a drug addict, a felon, and a womanizer (so many fiancees, 5 kids with 5 different women etc) needs to be put on a pedestal as a hero and martyr for dying at the hands of police. Statues are made of him, a special corner in Minneapolis is made for him. Again, GOD HELP US!

Another case in Brooklyn Center, Minnesota that caused businesses to burn with the incident where an 18 or so year old African American was pulled over for having something hanging from his rearview mirror.

The female cop ran his license and realized he had missed his court date so she tried to arrest him but he started pushing on the gas so the car could get away. This caused the female officer to fear for her and her partner's life so she was going to grab her taser, but accidentally in a split second accidentally grabbed her gun by mistake and shot and killed the 18 year old.

Her partner was going to be hurt or killed by the moving car. One certain community seemed apt on putting her in jail for a split second decision and an accident. Honestly, she shouldn't have spent any time in jail. It was an accident and had the kid just allowed and manned up to what he did by simply letting the cop arrest him, he'd still be alive.

How the 18 year olds mother and father praised their son. His mom said what a good, upstanding citizen he was. He actually missed his court date that they were going to arrest him on, on purpose. If he were my kid I'd consider myself a failure as a mother. Though that is just me. I hope to and will do SO much better as a parent.

He had shot and paralyzed someone and didn't have the "balls" to face what he did. That person will live the rest of their lives in a wheelchair due to that 18 year old's action. Yes, he was a terrible coward but his mom will say he was a good, upstanding citizen. That is such a load of CRAP!

The officer spent time in prison and is trying to rebuild her life. Unfortunately, the mother of the 18 year old that preaches that her son was such a great person, just cannot let it go and let this woman be. The former police officer has paid more than her debt to society. They actually threw her under a bus when it happened. No one deserves that. Let her go on with her life. The son was really no angel.

Just as in the case on Memorial Day, the cop was caucasian and the victim was African American. For some reason, if it is a cop of the same race as a person they have shot, it is okay. The media will only mention it for like 5 seconds.

However, when the cop is Caucasian and the person they had to shoot is African American, there is an excess amount of media claiming racism even though there is no proof. The liars in the media will blow up the story so much it will cause riots, burning, and mass protests.

However, the media is simply into sensationalizing stories and not reporting on the whole story. They take tidbits and feed it to us. They just want ratings. They really don't give a shit about reporting the whole truth. Honestly, I don't even watch the news or read it online or in the newspaper.

MY FINAL THOUGHTS

I was never taught to consistently stick with something so that I would eventually succeed. If I failed, I was simply a failure. No one is a failure, unless they stop trying. I was never encouraged to keep trying to succeed at anything. I know differently now.

If I failed, it was just something I couldn't do. I was taught that failure is a personal thing, not something that has to be overcome and eventually triumphed. That is something I'm really trying to overcome. Failure is simply part of the process, it is not an ending.

Life has peaks and valleys. It's how you celebrate the peaks, enjoy the view and overcome the valleys and climb back to the top. I am responsible for myself and my behavior. No one or societal entity forces me to do or not do something.

I make those choices and implement them. If I break a law, there are consequences for that action. Every behavior has equal consequences and an equal reaction. We may not be responsible for everything that happens in our lives but we do have the responsibility and power on how we react to it.

I have choices and fully believe those choices affect my life, so I choose carefully. Yes, a lot of trauma happened in my life but I choose how to view it and move on. I have power over me and that is really important to recognize.

People remember how you treat them. Those who have mistreated me, I have never forgotten. I'll forgive and move on, but I will never forget.

I value my friends and if it works out with the server, I will be forever grateful. The guy is so epic and he "gets" me. I know that is so rare as I'm a square peg in a round hole. Lord knows I've paid so much for being different but it has made me so strong.

Practicing gratitude makes us appreciate what we have and can make life so much happier. I have found that being thankful for what I have makes a real difference in my life because it can all be taken away in an instant.

Being around positive people makes a huge difference as well. My work friends and friends I've kept in touch with

over the years mean the world to me. I wouldn't trade them for anything. For years I was stuck with toxic, energy sucking people who were all about themselves.

I never said "no" to things and now I take better care of my energy and myself. It's important to take care of one's needs. I didn't learn this until much later in life. Saying "no" didn't even seem like an option for me as I had never put myself first. I learned to put my needs ahead of others.' If I don't take care of myself and my personal needs, no one else will.

Sometimes in life we need to say "no" to protect ourselves and our wellbeing. I've learned it's okay and to put myself first. If I don't take care of myself and my needs, I won't be any help to others.

I'm still looking for a hobby. I really love acting and I will pursue this as a side gig. I highly doubt that I will ever become "famous" or "known" in the industry but I do love the craft. I need to meet more people in person, but I have yet to discover the best way to do that.

I have been taken advantage of and used so much that it is really hard for me to trust people-especially people I haven't met before. Trust is a very important and fundamental part of a relationship. Some of the people I trusted most in my life have done horrible things to me. It's not something I take lightly in life. Trust once broken is never the same again.

HUMAN UNDERSTANDING

We are all so human! Imagine if we saw each other as simply humans trying to do their best in life. What if we gave each other a break, empathy and understanding. What if we weren't defined by the party we voted for, being a race, man, woman or based on who we love? What if we defined ourselves as simply the "human race." Imagine what would happen.

I'm telling you what I'm going to do as this is a somewhat long story and I appreciate your taking the time to read it. I'm so grateful.

As I am doing, I'm going to try to be the best version of myself I can be everyday. I'm going to make mistakes, have challenges, mess up and sometimes things will be epically hard. I know! It's life and life is pain as I had mentioned before.

I'm not going to make servers, retail workers, coffee house workers (anyone who works with the public) hurt because I do. That is not fair and pain simply doesn't need to be spread. There is enough in each individual human life. I'm going to treat them with respect and dignity. Every human should be treated that way.

Lord knows the person who sits in that corner office who makes some epically shitty decisions that cause the people at the bottom who make so little money and need those jobs, headaches, frustration and anger. But those people are my heroes as I have been and I am in their shoes.

The person in that comfy corner office with a great view doesn't make the country run. Those on the front lines taking orders, filling shelves, and doing the hard work do. You see, the most important person in a business is the one dealing with the customer, holding their tongue when some asshole wants to complain, bitch, piss and moan about something. The person in that corner office, with a great view and an MBA, doesn't see the people at the bottom as human. They are wages and cost money. To cut hours to save money doesn't affect those at corporate.

To cut hours of the people at corporate or forced vacations for a couple of weeks is just too much for the people at corporate. They, after all, depend on their salary. Gosh! Thing is, so do those at the bottom doing all the hard work. Their jobs are their livelihood on so many levels.

The people at the corporate level can afford to take an unpaid day here and there to save the company money. The genius in the corner office, who doesn't have a brain, can't figure THAT out. After all, they do have an MBA and no common sense.

God forbid someone consider another human has feelings. Then again, I grew up with epically selfish people so I know that there are way too many people like that in the world…sadly.

Again, thank you for reading this. Again, I'm so grateful. If my experience can save anyone from the epic amounts of pain of my life up to this point, I've done my job. I love people. I always have. They just tend to tire me out after a while and I need solitude and quiet to center myself. Afterall, I'm an introvert and that is how we recharge.

I'm going to continue to live strong, proud and sticking up for myself and other human beings. It's just who I am. I hope you make the same choice. There are some epically shitty people out there and they do need to know that their actions affect other people and have consequences. Unfortunately, Mom never learned that.

Please teach those horrible, awful, unhappy people that is not acceptable on any level. Let's try to, again, see each other as the "human race" and see what happens. I'll tell you what, I'll be brave and go first. I sure hope you will follow.